Myths of the Cold War

Myths of the Cold War

Amending Historiographic Distortions

Albert L. Weeks

LEXINGTON BOOKS
Lanham • Boulder • New York • London

Published by Lexington Books
An imprint of Rowman & Littlefield
4501 Forbes Boulevard, Suite 200, Lanham, Maryland 20706
www.rowman.com

16 Carlisle Street, London W1D 3BT, United Kingdom

Copyright © 2014 by Lexington Books

All rights reserved. No part of this book may be reproduced in any form or by any electronic or mechanical means, including information storage and retrieval systems, without written permission from the publisher, except by a reviewer who may quote passages in a review.

British Library Cataloguing in Publication Information Available

Library of Congress Cataloging-in-Publication Data

Weeks, Albert Loren, 1923–
Myths of the Cold War : amending historiographic distortions / Albert L. Weeks.
p. cm.
Includes bibliographical references and index.
ISBN 978-0-7391-8969-6 (cloth) — ISBN 978-0-7391-8970-2 (electronic)
1. Cold War—Historiography. 2. United States—Foreign relations—Soviet Union. 3. Soviet Union—Foreign relations—United States. I. Title.
D847.W44 2014
909.82'5072—dc23

2014015135

∞ ™ The paper used in this publication meets the minimum requirements of American National Standard for Information Sciences Permanence of Paper for Printed Library Materials, ANSI/NISO Z39.48-1992.

Printed in the United States of America

In memory of a steadfast friend, Frederick Duda

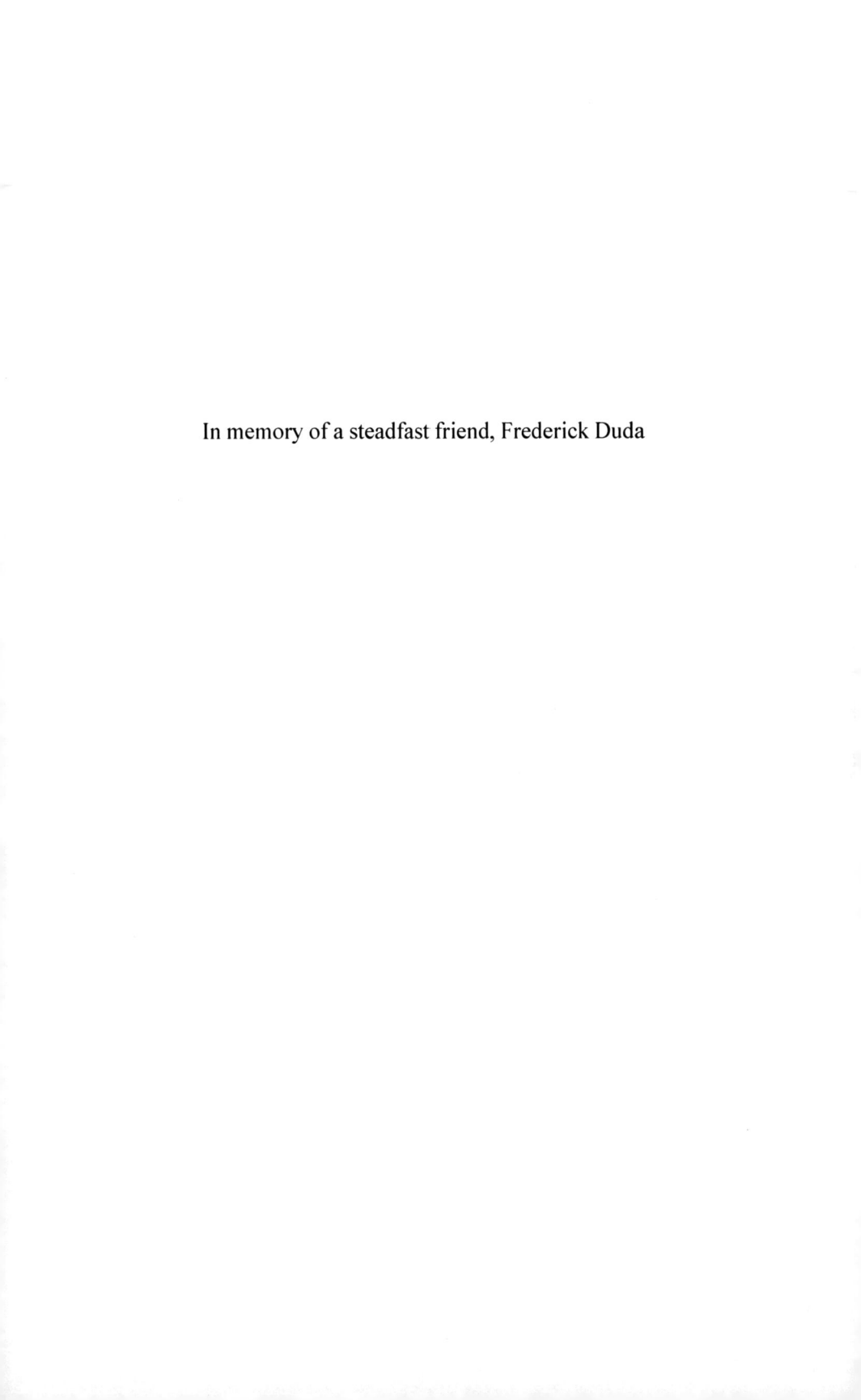

Contents

Preface		ix
1	Introduction: Distorted Cold War Historiography	1
2	Cold War Basics	19
3	The Myth of "Ideological Irrelevance"	33
4	Fallacy of Stalin's "Defencist" Security	55
5	Cold War Clash Over a Postwar World	97
6	Current Russian Texts on the Cold War	109

Myths of the Cold War　　　　　　　　　　　　　　　　　117
　Albert L. Weeks

Molotov's and Stalin's Electoral Speeches　　　　　　　　121

Soviet Communist Party Secretary Andrei Zhdanov's "Two-
　Camp" Cold War Speech, January 16, 1948　　　　　　127

Bibliography　　　　　　　　　　　　　　　　　　　　131

About the Author　　　　　　　　　　　　　　　　　143

Preface

ABOUT THIS BOOK

My book has been inspired by the plethora of recent titles on the U.S.–Soviet Cold War. This writer, a so-called "cold warrior," worked as a Russian-reading Senior Soviet Analyst for the U.S. Department of State's International Broadcasting Division as well as for Radio Free Europe at the height of the Cold War (1950–1956) For me, tackling this topic was like flying in a helicopter over familiar territory.

In the current abundant literature on the Cold War, we are witnessing what appears to me in some cases to be a lamentable historiographic distortion of this forty-five year long struggle. In reviewing the main essentials of the Cold War—but by no means here writing another history of the struggle—this writer has tried in the coming chapters to hew to standards of objectivity. There is no attempt in my book to "black ball" certain writers, to impute a "pro-Communist" or "anti-American" taint to their writings. In finding misinterpretation and misrepresentation in their works, this writer, obviously, does not mean that readers should avoid reading and pondering the contents of such books. The issue of U.S. involvement in the Cold War is simply too complex for any one observer to set up oneself as an all-seeing judge. I hope only to open an avenue for discussion.

In canvassing a large body of Cold War literature, I have discovered that the contents of some of these print or aired presentations err both by omission and commission. Some of the revisionist issues may stem from ideological pretensions on the part of the authors or documentary producers. Other tendentiousness involves some authors' disposition to place the blame for the Cold War on what they regard as the arrogant possessor of "preponderant power," namely, the American "imperial" superpower. They thus downgrade in importance the triggering of the Cold War by Stalin's contentious policies and the dogmatic ideology. Other problems in Cold War literature stem from writers' lack of a knowledge of the Russian language.

Readers of my book should not expect to find a thoroughgoing history the U.S.–Soviet Cold War. For example, there is no exposition here of the postwar problem of Germany; no year-by-year summary of the Cold War based on exhaustive examination of official documents. For this, a number of excellent published surveys exist: for example, works by E.H. Carr,

Adam Ulam, Max Beloff, or John L. Gaddis. Instead of such comprehensiveness, this book presents a brief critique of a selected number of Cold War authors and their interpretations. What is crucial, in my view, are the criteria and the relevant interpretations, the authors' selection (or not) of supporting factual material, and their overarching historiography philosophy that have evidently motivated some of these authors.

Singling out particular Cold War issues is the motivation on my part to help better understand the anatomy of the past Cold War. In the forthcoming chapters, I hope to throw light on the mainsprings and essential meaning of the Cold War together with the shortcomings in the interpretation of this titanic, $4 trillion struggle. By so doing, I hope the analysis might help encourage a better coping with the anatomy of any "next" cold war. I approach this historiographic issue of "Present Interest" in the last chapter.

January 2014

ONE
Introduction: Distorted Cold War Historiography

Disagreement and confusion over the U.S.-Soviet Cold War are such that few authors who discuss that dangerous era can agree on fundamentals like:

What started the Cold War.
When it started and how long it lasted.
Who or what was responsible for it.
Whether such dangerous, expensive cold-war type interstate conflicts can be prevented.

To appreciate how extreme the controversy has become, consider the following disagreements between leading Cold War authors (duly cited in later chapters; Russian authors and titles are listed separately in chapter 6):[1]

- The United States was the principal cause of the Cold War since that country, bandying about a "preponderance of power" and the atomic weapon, sought global domination ("hegemony") and sowed hostility toward the USSR after World War II—*versus*—Soviet imperialist ideology imbedded in Marxism-Leninism guided the foreign policies developed by Lenin (1917–24), Stalin (1925–1953), and their successors up to the demise of the USSR (1991). Ideology was employed and imbedded in practice in foreign policy by the Kremlin to justify violation of independent nations' sovereignty in the name of "extending the frontiers of socialism"; it also served as an indispensable prop for the party-state dictatorship (see discussion on ideology in chapter 3). As Gorbachev described Soviet power in a BBC interview in March 2012: "A responsible state power should appreciate its own country's sovereign interests as well as those of its neighbors along with international concerns. [In eastern Europe] I am accused of having given those countries away. But whom did I give them to? I gave Poland, for example, back to the Poles. Whom else does Poland belong to?"

- Whereas the administration of Franklin D. Roosevelt (1933–1945) sought friendship with Stalin's Soviet Union, even to the point of calling Stalinist Soviet Russia a type of democracy (see discussion in forthcoming chapters and in appendix I), the Truman administration, which succeeded FDR's in spring 1945, intentionally sought a hostile relationship with the Soviets. Truman's "ruling circles" joined forces with "reactionary bourgeois imperialist elements" seeking to protect the capitalist system in Western Europe while asserting U.S. global hegemony by demonizing and "containing" progressive forces represented by Stalin, the USSR, and Western Communist Parties—*versus*—Truman's succession to Roosevelt came at the time of heightened Soviet expansionism in eastern Europe following signs of a serious falling out between Stalin and Roosevelt, shortly before he died, over Poland and other issues; these were problems Truman inherited after April 1945. How FDR would have handled them is anyone's guess. Some of FDR's closest associates by 1946 were deeply disillusioned by Soviet behavior.

Perception during the Roosevelt Administration of the onset of Soviet expansionism is evident, for example, in the recollections of other such participants in meetings with Stalin and his closest aides as Gen. John R. Deane and Gen. Walter Bedell Smith.[2] More familiar accounts and analyses by major participants in such encounters by Kennan, Harriman, and in the post-Roosevelt period, James F. Byrnes, President Harry F. Truman et al., are referenced in coming chapters. A small minority of Russian historians (see chapter 5) are critical of Stalin's role as initiator of the Cold War.[3]

George F. Kennan complained about Roosevelt's naïveté about Stalin and Soviet intentions. If more nuanced than Deane's and without reference to a Soviet "war" against capitalism, in his famous *Foreign Affairs* essay July 1947 he warned of Soviet perfidy.[4] The 1979 House committee study on U.S.-Soviet relations after the war, cited above, concluded: "Clearly, the signs were ominous [after World War II] for the future conduct of diplomacy and negotiations with the Soviet Union." At least, it might be added, as long as the USSR was led by Josef Stalin. Rather typical of early revisionist treatment of the Cold War by American authors was the late Stephen E. Ambrose's contribution to the history of the war and its aftermath.[5] The British television series *World at War* was characterized by a pacifist emphasis and a tendentious, revisionist position on Stalin and the Cold War. This line reflected Ambrose's and the

British producers' personal thinking. He was of the revisionist school and of the U.S.-to-blame-cum-plague-on-both-houses historiography on the Cold War. His line of analysis followed and/or anticipated that of works by Henry Steele Commager, Frederick L. Schuman, Gar Alperovitz, Gabriel Kolko, William Appleton Williams, Mary Glantz, Joseph E. Davies, Geoffrey Roberts, and others. Their views are canvassed in coming chapters.[6]

- One such pro-Soviet document was the OWI/War Department booklet titled *The USSR: Institutions and People: A Brief Handbook for the Use of Officers of the Army of the United States*.[7] This was a long discussion in the widely-distributed U.S. Army enlisted personnel's orientation handbook. It reflected some of OWI personnel's known involvement in Soviet espionage and agents of influence, described in the Venona decrypts. These men and women acted in Washington, D.C. and catered to U.S. public vulnerability to such expressions of "soft power" from Stalin's Kremlin.[8]
- Symptomatic of how much the U.S.-Soviet relationship had soured justafter the war was ex-Prime Minister Winston Churchill's inflammatory "iron curtain" speech of March 1946 in Fulton, MO, that "shocked" Stalin—*versus*—the earlier, ominous electoral speeches made by Stalin and Molotov in February 1946 in which the two top Soviet leaders virtually declared a new war on the West (see appendix II for excerpts from the electoral speeches of Stalin and Molotov in February 1946).[9] The latter is the never-cited in Cold War literature electoral speech by Deputy Premier Vyacheslav Molotov, February 6. It carried the same ominous notes as Stalin's electoral address, in which Stalin claimed on the basis of Marxism-Leninism that World War II had stemmed from the "second crisis of capitalism," or its inevitable "aggressive" phase.[10] This reference to inveterately embedded in Western capitalism as the prime case of war, including a future war, was regarded as ominous when it was reported in foreign coverage of Stalin's speech. No war, Stalin continued, "can ever arise accidentally." The Soviet Communist system had saved the USSR and had liberated other countries he said: "The Soviet social order is better than any non-Soviet system in the world." The past war was won by Soviet "active defense," suggesting that military preparedness was now a postwar necessity for the USSR (this attitude strongly contrasted with the generally Western official attitude that disarmament, demobilization, and reconstruction were now central concerns for the Allied Western countries). Without heavy industry, Stalin said, Soviet defenses could not be built up: "To lag behind in emphasizing heavy industry means to lose and bring about the destruction of the Soviet

system. [Such a buildup] will guarantee the safety of our country from any future contingencies."

For his part, Molotov, whom one of the Western revisionists praises for his alleged non-ideological "realism" (see chapter 3) noted that the postwar Five-Year Plan would result in the Soviets' "overtaking and surpassing economically the most highly-developed European capitalist countries as well as the United States of America. [This] will be accomplished in the nearest future." Soviet foreign policy, he said accusingly, will keep the "aggressor pack chained." This is why the Soviet Union is vigilant when it comes to possible centers of violating the peace and international security or to any intrigues along those lines. The government and the leadership of the Soviet Army are doing what is necessary to ensure that the very latest types of armaments, our Army will not be inferior to that of any other country." Soviet participation in the United Nations "is aimed at preventing fresh wars and curbing all and every imperialist aggressor" (emphases mine—ALW). He boasted that the Soviet victory in the East had guaranteed that the USSR would be ranked "among the world powers. Important problems in international relations henceforth cannot be settled without the participation of the Soviet Union. The participation of Comrade Stalin [in such affairs] is regarded as the best guarantee of a successful resolution of complicated international problems." He noted that the strategy used in the war "was under the immediate guidance of Comrade Stalin, our great Army leader."

Milovan Djilas, in *Conversations with Stalin*, relates how Stalin told him in Moscow in 1945 during the Yugoslav top official's tête-à-tête with the Soviet dictator that the USSR will have "another go at it" to defeat the capitalists in a future war.[11]

Of the many books on the Cold War, and they run to the many dozens, perhaps the best and most objective among the most recent is John L. Gaddis, *The Cold War: A New History*. Lamentably, however, all these books ignore the Duclos letter as well as the symptomatic purging in early 1945 of Browder as General Secretary of the world's most important Communist Party, the CPUSA. Both events signaled an emerging hard line from the Kremlin.[12] The transition from cold to hot war with North Korea's invasion of the south in June 1950 is analyzed in Haynes and Klehr's *Venona*.

In the Far East, Stalin gave encouragement in Korea to Chinese participation instead of direct Soviet involvement in the fighting. Which suggests an old Chinese saying: *"Chie dao sha jen,"* or "borrowing a knife to kill another." In these materials Stalin is found declaring the Far East to be the post war's "new center of revolution" in which the Soviets' "junior partner," China, would play a leading role—under Soviet guidance. As to the danger of a Third

World War's possibly stemming from the conflict in Korea, the Soviet leader stated frankly just five years after the bloody world war: *"If war is inevitable, let it be waged now, and not in a few years when Japanese militarism will be restored as an ally of the USA and when the USA and Japan have a ready-made bridgehead in the form of the entire Korea run by Syngman Rhee."* For his part, Mao offered the opinion in early 1950 that the United States was "afraid of war" and would not intervene in Korea. For his part, Stalin declared that the Korean War showed "America's weakness."

- In the Venona papers (see citation above), Browder is described by the NKVD as a Moscow tool but who has become a liability to Moscow by 1944–1945. For one thing, his ambitious plan to create a broad, appeasing left-wing arm of the Democratic Party in the form of a so-called Communist-run "Political Association" was vetoed in Moscow. It appears that Stalin wished to retain the purity of the Communist Party, not see it morphed and adulterated into a putatively non-Communist entity. Browder had also been personally involved in some embarrassing incidents (for the NKVD) that might have exposed other agents. This would include persons whom Browder himself had recruited for the NKVD via the CPUSA. As CPUSA General Secretary, Browder had been bitterly criticized by top French Communist Party official, Jacques Duclos, in his famous 1945 letter. The Venona espionage documents reveal that Browder enjoyed friendly, personal ties with President Roosevelt, which in turn may have been viewed in Moscow as a mixed benefit.[13]

- On the ominous signs of a coming cold war, ambassador to the USSR George F. Kennan, in his famous July 1947 *Foreign Affairs* essay, made a number of observations, if somewhat more nuanced than Deane's and without reference to an actual Soviet "war" against capitalism.[14] The 1979 House committee study on U.S.-Soviet relations after the war concluded: "Clearly, the signs were ominous [after World War II] for the future conduct of diplomacy and negotiations with the Soviet Union." At least, it might be added, as long as the USSR was led by Josef Stalin. Rather typical of early revisionist treatments of the Cold War by American authors was the late author, Stephen E. Ambrose's contribution to the history of the war and its aftermath. He helped write for the British *World at War* TV series, narrated by Laurence Olivier. This series was characterized by a pacifist emphasis and a tendentious, revisionist position on Stalin and the Cold War. The leftist line reflected Ambrose's personal thinking. Revisionist-inclined or outright apologetic or U.S.-to-blame-cum-plague-on-both-houses histories or memoirs written up to the present include works by Henry Steele Commager, Frederick L. Schuman, Gar Alperovitz, Gabriel Kolko, William

Appleton Williams, Mary Glantz, Joseph E. Davies, Geoffrey Roberts, and others. Such views are canvassed in coming chapters.
- Contingency war planning is, of course, the commonly-used prerogative of any state. It was especially true of the two atomic powers, the USSR and the United States by the mid-1940s. Moscow as well as Washington did such planning. Moscow's own plans were detailed in various sources. One popular account was reported in the British newspaper, *Telegraph*, on September 20, 2007, which read "Soviet Plan for World War III Unearthed." Bona fide Russian defectors, especially those with security backgrounds, have disclosed details of these Soviet war plans. U.S. and British plans against the Soviet Union bore such names as "Dropshot" and "Unthinkable." Strategic Air Command General Curtis LeMay, ironically a wartime recipient of the Soviet "Great Patriotic War" medal, was often accused of planning a nuclear attack against the USSR. Post-Soviet Russian historian A. B. Martirosyan accuses Gen. Dwight D. Eisenhower of supporting the "Anglo-Saxon elite" in their plan to attack the USSR under the alleged code-name, "Totality." Other supposedly less extreme Russian historians, who have had their works translated into foreign languages including English, have written about such U.S. war plans accusing the United States of postwar aggressiveness. These Russian authors are some of the most widely read in their own country and abroad. They include among others mainline historians or memoirists like Lev Bezymensky, Oleg Rzheshevsky, Valentin Falin, and Yuri Zhukov.
- Further symbolic of the way U.S.-Soviet relationship soured just after the war was ex-Prime Minister Winston Churchill's "iron curtain" speech of March 1946 in Fulton, MO, that "shocked" Stalin—*versus*—the earlier, ominous electoral speeches made by Stalin and Molotov in February 1946 in which the two top Soviet leaders virtually declared a new war on the West (see appendix II for excerpts from the electoral speeches of Stalin and Molotov in February 1946). never-cited in Cold War literature electoral speech by Deputy Premier Vyacheslav Molotov, February 6. It carried the same ominous notes as Stalin's electoral address, in which Stalin claimed on the basis of Marxism-Leninism that World War II had stemmed from the "second crisis of capitalism," or its inevitable "aggressive" phase.[15] This reference to inveterately embedded in Western capitalism as the prime case of war, including a future war, was regarded as ominous when it was reported in foreign coverage of Stalin's speech. No war, Stalin continued, "can ever arise accidentally." The Soviet Communist system had saved the USSR and had liberated other countries he said: "The Soviet social order is better than any non-Soviet system in the world." The past war was won by Soviet "active defense," suggesting that military preparedness

was now a postwar necessity for the USSR (this attitude strongly contrasted with the generally Western official attitude that disarmament, demobilization, and reconstruction were now central concerns for the Allied Western countries). Without heavy industry, Stalin said, Soviet defenses could not be built up: "To lag behind in emphasizing heavy industry means to lose and bring about the destruction of the Soviet system. [Such a buildup] will guarantee the safety of our country from any future contingencies."

For his part, Molotov, whom one of the Western revisionists praises for his alleged non-ideological "realism" (see chapter 3) noted that the postwar Five-Year Plan would result in the Soviets' "overtaking and surpassing economically the most highly-developed European capitalist countries as well as the United States of America. [This] will be accomplished in the nearest future." Soviet foreign policy, he said accusingly, will keep the "aggressor pack chained." This is why the Soviet Union is vigilant when it comes to possible centers of violating the peace and international security or to any intrigues along those lines. The government and the leadership of the Soviet Army are doing what is necessary to ensure that the very latest types of armaments, our Army will not be inferior to that of any other country." Soviet participation in the United Nations "is aimed at preventing fresh wars and curbing all and every imperialist aggressor" (emphases mine—ALW). He boasted that the Soviet victory in the East had guaranteed that the USSR would be ranked "among the world powers. Important problems in international relations henceforth cannot be settled without the participation of the Soviet Union. The participation of Comrade Stalin [in such affairs] is regarded as the best guarantee of a successful resolution of complicated international problems." He noted that the strategy used in the war "was under the immediate guidance of Comrade Stalin, our great Army leader."

- Perception of such continuation of traditional Soviet aggression towards the West is also evident, for example, in the recollections of other such participants in meetings with Stalin and his closest aides as Gen. John R. Deane and Gen. Walter Bedell Smith.[16] More familiar accounts and analyses by major participants in such encounters by Kennan, Harriman, James F. Byrnes, President Harry S. Truman et al., are cited in coming chapters. Yet a small minority of Russian historians are likewise critical of Stalin's role as initiator of the Cold War. Cf., e.g., Yevgeniy Anisimov, op. cit.

- Soviet ideology thus stressed that the past war or any future war stems inevitably from the very nature of the capitalist system. In 1945, Stalin remarked to the No. 2 official in Communist Yugoslavia that "we'll have another go at it" in a future war with the capitalist West.

- For its part, the Soviet Union under Stalin after the war, it is suggested by some leftist Cold War writers, pursued a policy of harmless, traditionally "realist" defencism aimed at merely to enhancing Soviet external security on the east European "springboard" of past invasions of Russia. In their view, Soviet defencism had nothing to do with militant Marxism-Leninism, world-revolutionism, or Soviet territorial expansionism The emerging Cold War was engineered by U.S. "hawks" intent on rattling the America's newly-acquired A-bomb and practicing "A-bomb diplomacy" against the USSR. Meanwhile, it is claimed, the Americans were planning a preemptive attack on the USSR.[17] The Cold War is mistakenly portrayed by such writers as an "ideologically-based conflict"—*versus*—the view that Stalin's policy as one of deliberate expansionism propelled by Communist ideology coupled to deceptive exploitation of popular Western, particularly FDR's, hope of East-West cooperation after the war under the aegis of the United Nations Organization, established in 1946. Postwar Soviet policy, moreover, included an elaborate system of intrusive espionage against the United States together with Soviet government-sponsored adversarial propaganda in Soviet media. Factually, post-World War II Soviet spying became history's largest such operation aimed at subverting and stealing secrets from another country thereby violating a country's sovereign right to protection of its borders from hostile foreign intrusion.

The above are some of the contending views held toward the Cold War. To the left of the "versus" divider are views expressed to one degree or another by various contemporary Cold War authors, including a majority of Russian history texts. The claims made by some of these authors are simply bizarre. For instance, one well-known British author, writing on "Stalin's wars" and the biography of Stalin's number two aide, Vyacheslav Molotov, claims that the latter did not really deserve the reputation of being a rigid "Mr. Nyet" hardliner. Molotov, the said writer insists, was a Kissinger-like advocate of a traditionally realist, *non*-ideological *point d'appui* in the making of Soviet foreign policy. The writer, Geoffrey Roberts, suggests that Molotov did not really favor a traditional Marxist-Leninist worldview of Communist expansionism, and of "world revolution"—that is, loyalty to the Soviets' ruling ideology. Yet, alas, in Molotov's own memoirs, the retired interviewee, then in his eighties, boasts how The Leader, Stalin, successfully "extended the frontiers of socialism," especially during and after World War II. In other respects Molotov comes through as a totally-dedicated cold-warrior in the Soviet sense. Meanwhile, nearly every reputable, published authority on the Soviet leadership, when writing about Molotov—such writers include former Politburo comrades and almost all reputable Western specialists on the Soviet leadership—depict Molotov as the hardest, most ideological of Kremlin hardliners. Which is how American and British envoys and their government intelligence actually found him to be in their encounters with Molotov in London, Moscow, or Washington during and after the war. To depict Molotov as a sincere advocate of old-style Western "realist" diplomacy that is free of ideological pretension and aggressiveness is totally erroneous and, as Russians say, "sucked out of fingers."

The same author, described by a reputable Cold War author as a "staunch leftist," at times contrasts this alleged "rational" Molotovian approach with the West's show of undue "alarm" and "hysteria" over nonexistent Soviet expansionism, its militant ideology, and totalitarianism.[18] Such writers, who unfortunately are numerous, emphasize, moreover, Western governments' alleged contingency plans to "destroy the USSR." These paper projections—which were never fleshed out in any way—bore such names as "Operation Unthinkable" and "Drop Shot," both of which contingency plans were dismissed as impractical. Contingency war-planning is, of course, the commonly used prerogative of any state.

This planning and speculation were especially true of the two atomic powers, the USSR and the U.S. The former's own plans have been described in various sources. One popular account was reported in the British newspaper, *Telegraph*, on September 20, 2007, titled, "Soviet Plan for World War III Unearthed." Russian defectors, especially those with a police background, disclosed details of these Soviet war plans against the West. U.S. plans against the Soviet Union bore such names as "Dropshot." Strategic Air Command General Curtis LeMay, ironically a wartime recipient of the Soviet "Great Patriotic War" medal, was often accused of planning a nuclear attack against the USSR. For example, a post-Soviet historian, A. B. Martirosyan, who appears to be in the Putin circle of historians, accuses Gen. Dwight D. Eisenhower of supporting the "Anglo-Saxon elite" in their plan to attack the USSR under the alleged codename, "Totality." Some Western Cold War authors cite these discarded, paper contingency speculations in the context of a dire, American assertion of its "preponderance of power." Other less extreme, Russian historians have written about such U.S. war plans accusing the United States of unwarranted aggressiveness. These Russian authors are some of the most widely read in their own country and abroad. They include, among others mainline historians or memoirists like Lev Bezymensky, Oleg Rzheshevsky, Valentin Falin, and Yuri Zhukov, who have been translated into English.

The anti-West line by some Cold War writers is particularly salient in works by quasi-Marxist, leftist writers as well as by Soviet and post-Soviet apologist-historians in Putin's Russia. They exempt Kremlin behavior during the Cold War mainly because, they claim, of the "baseless suspicious" of anti-Soviet "Anglo-Saxons."

Some astute Western writers recount how naive President Roosevelt and his immediate circle were about Stalin and the Soviets, As Anne Applebaum has written:[19] "Particularly towards the end of his life] Roosevelt frequently expressed his faith in Stalin's good intentions. 'Don't worry,' he told the Polish exile leader Stanislaw Mikolajczyk in 1942, 'Stalin doesn't intend to take freedom from Poland. He wouldn't dare do that because he knows that the United States government stands behind you.'" Another example. One author, whose book on FDR's policies during and after the war bears the subtitle *The President's Battles over Foreign Policy* singles out for criticism certain American officials, like George F. Kennan and others in the State Department (e.g., William C. Bullitt, Loy Henderson, or Robert F. Kelley).[20] These men, she vehemently claims, deliberately spoiled the chance of an amicable, bilateral U.S.-Soviet future that FDR and the Soviets, including Stalin and Molotov, hoped would materialize after the war. U.S.-Soviet friendship did not happen, she laments. Instead, the Cold War set in. The author insists this happened because of hawkish, "bureaucratic resistance" in Washington against a live-and-let-live Rooseveltian policy that would have, she implies, prevented the outbreak of the conflict.

Other notorious distortions of the Cold War currently turn up in print and air media. Various video documentaries on World War II and its aftermath display various forms of tendentiousness. For instance, whenever a given documentary discusses the Soviet-perpetrated Katyn Massacre of 22,000 Polish officers, incarcerated by the Soviets in 1940, it is rarely if ever pointed out how vehemently Moscow denied (even in the post-Soviet period) any Soviet involvement in the murders of these Polish officers nor how the Roosevelt Administration took Soviet denials of complicity seriously, despite Polish eye-witness reports to the contrary. Belatedly, in the 1990s, official Soviet documents surfaced in Moscow after years of repeated Kremlin denial over the existence of such documents. The evidence plainly showed Stalin's own signature on an ukase issued in spring 1940 to "liquidate" the imprisoned Poles. Nor is it pointed out in conventional Western coverage of Katyn how the Roosevelt Administration supported the Soviet line that the massacre story was only a piece of German propaganda. To have assumed Soviet guilt would have supposedly sullied the chances of U.S.-Soviet friendship, which hope stood at the core of Roosevelt's policy toward the USSR.

Another instance of less-than-the-truth coverage of events by Western authors or the producers and writers of wartime and postwar documentaries that bear upon events leading up to the Cold War concerns the Warsaw Uprising that lasted sixty-three days after November 1944. At that time, thousands of members of the native Polish resistance Home Army sought to liberate their capital. The uprising was specifically timed to the Soviet Army's presumed preparation to invade Poland. Soviet Army divisions were poised just outside Warsaw's suburbs ready to attack. Moreover, Stalin had appealed to the Warsaw Poles to rise and drive out the Nazi occupiers and tormentors, a fact that is rarely if ever pointed out in the literature or in documentaries on this tragic event. Stalin deceptively halted the Soviet Army just outside Warsaw. He refused to let Western aircraft drop supplies to the Polish Home Army fighting the Nazis in Warsaw. In briefly skirting these events, some Cold War authors ignore altogether the fact that Stalin had *originally* appealed to the Warsaw rebels to fight for liberation. Instead, one writer mistakenly claims the Warsaw Home Army had "no contact" with Moscow or the "Red" (he means Soviet). The grim consequence of Stalin's trickery was that the poorly armed Polish freedom fighters were no match for the Nazi weaponry. As the Soviet Army stood idle, hundreds of thousands of heroic young and older Poles were gunned down in a virtual massacre.

It was clear, of course, why Stalin let this happen, a motivation that perturbed Western leaders at the time but who nevertheless chose not to make an issue out of it with Stalin. The fact was the Soviet dictator was preparing his own Polish occupation force. He was planning to export Sovietism, as the expression goes, "on the tips of bayonets," a phrase actually used in Red Army propaganda of the 1920s. The Soviet-run occupation of Poland was to be composed of so-called "Lublin Poles," or Communist Quislings based and trained in the USSR. It was they, not any native Polish movement or the émigré London Poles, who would compose the ruling core that took over Poland as Soviet gauleiters.

This Soviet fraud was in violation of the principles of the Atlantic Charter, the Declaration on the Liberation of Europe and other legal documents providing for democratic rule in eastern Europe to which the USSR formally—and hypocritically—subscribed. The Soviet-trained Polish Quislings set about converting this largest east European neighbor of Russia into a full-fledged Communist-ruled, totalitarian satellite. It was established on the model of the twenty-year old Mongolian People's Republic under a Soviet dictatorship in 1924. Its title and description as a "People's Democracy" became a standby with the Maoists, who borrowed the Soviet phraseology of "People's Republic." This terminology was applied to Communist China just as Moscow had first applied it to its east European satellites beginning in 1944–45. The North Korean Communists call their state the "Democratic People's Republic of Korea," omitting, of course, the qualifying expression "North." The Pyongyang regime considers its government to be the only legitimate one for the entire Korean Peninsula. Its party program includes the aim to unify the peninsula by putting it under Communist rule.

At the time, the Roosevelt Administration reacted only mildly to this outrage in Poland (and later in Romania) as a violation of Big Three agreements at Yalta and Potsdam as well as of other agreements. Instead, Washington formally supported the Soviet pretext of not helping the Polish resisters in Warsaw. The Administration endorsed Kremlin propaganda that an invasion of the capital city was not "timely." The Kremlin leaders were not criticized for standing idle as the decimation of the non-Communist resistance in Poland played out so brutally in the streets of Warsaw. Ambassador Standley, op. cit., wrote critically of Washington's mild reaction to Stalin's trickery over the Polish Home Army's decimation in Warsaw in 1945, which the Soviets had encouraged and then treacherously abandoned, before the Soviet Army itself "liberated" the Polish capital.

In some of the Cold War literature, authors claim that it was not Stalin who was behind such hard-line policies. It was, they claimed, his hard-line Politburo comrades "to whom Stalin was beholden." (Ambassador Standley critically addressed this myth, op. cit., pp. 213–14.) This preposterous notion was also proffered by a byline Washington newspaper reporter and others. They claimed that Stalin, or "Uncle Joe," was "a prisoner in the Kremlin."[21] This view was duly taken up in turn by various print-media editorialists. They insisted that Stalin himself was reasonable and tractable. It was only his colleagues who were the militantly ant-West. Even as astute a diplomat with experience as Ambassador to the USSR, Averell Harriman, could say: "Whenever Stalin gets tough with us, it's the Politburo attitude he's expressing, not his own views on the major subject at issue"

Cold War authors tend to ignore or downgrade the most revealing instances of Stalin's hypocrisy. One example was the dictator's contrived attitude toward the U.S. development of an A-bomb in 1945 and its use in ending the war with Japan in August 1945. The Soviet aim here was to attempt to deflate U.S. prestige and its power to subdue militaristic Japan with the two U.S. A-bomb attacks. Stalin's Soviet Army was deemed to be the main destroyer on Japanese militarism.

Another ruse was the Stalin regime's concealment of the fact that Soviet security forces had located Hitler's remains near the bunker in Berlin in May 1945. Instead of disclosing this discovery (which included Hitler's jaw bone and teeth and part of his skull, which the Soviets secretly kept in their possession), the Kremlin circulated inflammatory tales as to how Hitler (and his aide, Martin Bormann) were not really dead. They were still at large. The Soviet press alleged that elements in the West hoped to prepare a return to power of Hitlerite Fascism, whose elements they would employ against "progressive forces" in other countries. (This author knew any number of people after the war who believed in this fabricated story.)

In my over fifty years of college teaching, twenty of which were after 1991, I find that the prevailing campus attitude toward the Cold War, in part fostered by media and faculty, might best be summed up with the opinion that it was "much ado about nothing, a waste of money." John Prados, author of *How the Cold War Ended: Debating and Doing* concludes his lengthy catalog of opinions about the historic bipolar struggle with the puzzling statement that the U.S.-Soviet Cold War was an unnecessary, a zero-sum game:[22] "People everywhere [were losers and] found themselves crushed under the weight of a misbegotten conflict," he writes (p. 184) "Misbegotten"? Are all conflicts misbegotten, even World War II? The struggle to defeat totalitarian Fascism, Nazism, and Japanese militarism in that four-year shooting war was "misbegotten"?

Yet both hot and cold wars are known to have been fought over a *clash of principles*. All such conflicts, whether hot, cold, or "cool," cannot be summarily dismissed as unprincipled "zero-sum, games." Widespread campus opinion today apparently has it that as to the Cold War, probably "both sides" were equally to blame for its outbreak. Maybe superpower America was more to blame than the Soviets. At any rate, this is my impression of campus attitudes on the Cold War — on both sides of the teacher's desk. The impression, with few exceptions, is borne out by contemporary Cold War literature. It would be interesting to poll campuses on prevalent attitudes toward the Cold War.

Incidentally, the term "progressive forces" — that is, Communist-supported elements in Western countries — are described by some Cold War authors as devotees of "socially progressive patriotism." As mentioned above, whenever the blighted T-word describing the Soviet system is used, many Cold War authors place quotation marks around "totalitarianism": I have found that many college students cannot even pronounce this word. It's widely construed that a totalitarian system is merely fictitious, the invention of a writer like George Orwell. Speaking of such diacritical marks, some authors similarly demean expressions like Free World, Captive Nations, Freedom Fighters, even Western democracy by tendentiously putting quotation marks around these clearly denotative terms. Why they do this is anyone's guess.

A further distortion or omission by many revisionist or revisionist-inclined Cold War authors in their assessment of U.S.-Soviet relations during and after the war is seen in their assessment of American Lend-Lease aid extended to the Soviets beginning in 1942 and increasing in large amounts in 1943–1944.[23] The assistance had been had been promised by Western officials in conferences with Soviet officials, including Stalin, within days after the German invasion on June 22, 1941. Lend-Lease was once praised by Stalin and by Red Army commander Marshal Zhukov as an "indispensable" contribution to the Soviet war effort. However, after World War II, Stalin ordered a virtual silence in Soviet media about this $12.5 billion aid, or in terms of today's values, some one-quarter trillion dollars or more not to mention loss of ships and men in making the dangerous ocean crossings to ship the Lend-Lease goods. Whenever Lend-Lease was — and is — mentioned in Soviet and post-Soviet history texts, it was described as measly and inconsequential. Moreover, Soviet and post-Soviet authors mistakenly claimed that the aid composed only 4 percent of all Soviet war equipment. Later a few, courageous post-Soviet Russian scholars claimed that upwards to 25 percent of the most useful military technology used profitably on the Soviet side in combat was from Lend-Lease aid. This mauling of the truth was typical of the Soviet press and history during and after World War II. Unfortunately, such obfuscation is also found in books by a number of Cold War authors. Some do not even mention this aid.

To make sense out of the forty-plus year Cold War (one well-known author claims it lasted "fifty years," which would presumably take Cold War origins back to 1941).[24] Several causative factors need to be canvassed:

First, how seriously do we take repeated claims by Kremlin leaders—as voiced during World War II and even as late as the 1980s—that in winning the war on the Eastern Front, the Soviet Union was actively helping "liberate the working class worldwide"? It explicitly sought to make over the world in the Soviet image, and to do so by violent means. Or how do we regard the over dozen client-states worldwide established under Soviet guidance by the 1970s and Moscow's encouraging and arming "national-liberation wars" by creating geostrategic positions of "interdiction" via Soviet-built and -run naval and air bases at key points around the globe?[25]

What are we to make of the eighty-five or more countries that sent delegates to militant world conferences held in Moscow, Warsaw, or Bucharest that proclaimed a Soviet-type "socialist" future for the Third World and, in fact, for all countries? How do we interpret the notorious former Soviet support for terrorism? The best, well-documented source on Soviet support of global terrorism, a book generally ignored by Cold War writers or historians dealing with Soviet politics, is Albert Parry, *Terrorism from Robespierre to Arafat*.[26] Fluent in Russian, the late Dr. Parry did impressive research.

Incidentally, the revisionist trend in Sovietology and on the Cold War is described this way by Sarah Davies and James Harris (eds), op. cit, p. 3: "Until the 1960s, it was almost impossible to make any other interpretations in the U.S., at least [than the totalitarian model]. It was the changing political climate from the 1960s as well as changing social science methodologies, which fostered the development of revisionist challenges to the totalitarian orthodoxy." The authors seem to sympathize with this revisionist shift, still resonant in current literature on the Cold War. Some have attributed the latest post-1990's phase of revisionism and criticism of U.S. foreign policy to U.S. shortcomings or outright failures beginning with American-led wars in Vietnam, Iraq, and Afghanistan together with U.S. handling of the "Arab Spring" and the crisis in Syria of 2008–2013. Some Cold War authors appear to be guilty of the illogic of *post hoc, ergo propter hoc*. That is, they retrospectively draw conclusions about the Cold War based on present circumstances—that is, criticism of U.S. foreign policy of recent years, accusations of U.S. "global hegemony," and the putative decline in America's global standing.

Another motif has entered the discussion of cold wars and the U.S.-Soviet Cold War in particular. When the Russians, under Vladimir Putin's leadership, ordered Spetsnaz Special Forces into Crimea in early March 2014, the cry went up in the media and among some politicians that this was the beginning of a "new Cold War" with the Russians. The annexation of the Ukrainian peninsula or outright "aggression," as Secretary of State Kerry bluntly called it, could not be ignored. It was a blatant violation of the U.N. Charter and various documents of International Law that in recent years have established the inviolability of Ukraine's territorial sovereignty. Yet it is important to understand what this intrusion was not—at least so far. It was not among a string of deliberate, wholesale, Cold War-type violations of "near-abroad" national sovereignties of the kind Stalin engineered after World War II. Even Russia's former intrusion into the northern regions of Georgia that contain Muslim populations was not a full-fledged act of aggression, albeit a shocking piece of Bismarckian-type expansion, yet one that did not unduly upset RF-Georgian relations.

At this writing, it appeared the "Ukraine crisis" would not be resolved through agreement by the new Ukrainian government in Kiev and Western representatives on the one hand and the Russians on the other, with the result that there would be a new status for Crimea as a part of the RF. At the same time, salient were Russian concerns over the status of Crimea's naval assets as well as its pursuit of a broad "Eurasian" entity of some kind as proposed by Putin and his circle that would partly unify former Soviet-ruled parts in Central Asia and the Caucasus in both economic and geopolitical ways around a Russian core. Significantly, China presumably would not become an integral part of this entity despite the new entity's Asian extension. This, in turn, suggests that Russia seeks to erect as bridge under its supervision between East and West. From the West's standpoint, this might not be as "cold-warish" as it appears. For the Russian Federation may well be fashioning a geopolitical instrument by which it can act as a defensive wall, so to speak, against a "rising" China with seven times Russia's population. It also has a stronger economy and military than that of its northern non-Communist neighbor, whose departure from Sovietism and Communism is considered in Chinese textbooks to have been a "world-historical" mistake.

NOTES

1. Among the Cold War authors, their views, and their titles to be discussed, are: Gar Alperovitz, *Atomic Diplomacy: Hiroshima and Potsdam* (New York: Penguin Press, 1985); Melvyn P. Leffler, *For the Soul of Mankind: The United States and the Soviet Union and the Cold War* (New York: Hill and Wang, 2007); David S. Painter, *Origins of the Cold*

War (New York: Routledge, 1994); John Prados, *How the Cold War Ended: Debating and Doing History* (Washington, DC: Potomac Books, 2011); Norman Graebner et al., *America and the Cold War: A Realist Interpretation, 1941–1991* (New York: Praeger, 2010); Mary E. Glantz, *FDR and the Soviet Union: The President's Battles over Foreign Policy* (Lawrence: University Press of Kansas, 2005); Geoffrey Roberts, *Stalin's Wars: From World War to Cold War, 1939–1953* (New Haven, CT: Yale University Press, 2006); Roberts, *Molotov: Stalin's Cold Warrior* (Washington, DC: Potomac Books, 2012); John Lewis Gaddis, *We Now Know: Rethinking Cold War History* (Oxford: Clarendon Press, 1997); Gaddis, *George F. Kennan: An American Life* (New York: Penguin Books, 2011); Albert Resis, ed., *Molotov Remembers: Inside Kremlin Politics, Conversations with Felix Chuev* (Chicago: Ivan R. Dee, Chicago, 1997); Louis J. Halle, *The Cold War as History* (New York, Harper and Row, 1967); Norman E. Saul, *Friends or Foes? The United States and Russia, 1921–1941* (Lawrence: University of Press of Kansas, 2005); Yoram Gorlizki and Oleg Khlevniuk, *Cold Peace: Stalin and the Soviet Union's Ruling Circle, 1945–1953* (New York: Oxford University Press, 2004); Vladislav M. Zubok, *A Failed Empire: The Soviet Union in the Cold War from Stalin to Gorbachev* (Chapel Hill: University of North Carolina Press, 2007); D. F. Fleming, *The Cold War and Its Origins, 1917–1950*, vols. 1 and 2 (Garden City, NY: Doubleday, 1961); Vladislav Zubok and Constantine Pleshakov, *Inside the Kremlin's Cold War from Stalin to Khrushchev* (Cambridge, MA: Harvard University Press, 1996); Anne Applebaum, *Iron Curtain: The Crushing of Eastern Europe, 1944–1956* (New York: Penguin Books, 2012); Jussi M. Hanhimaki and Odd Arne Westad, *The Cold War: A History of Documents and Eyewitness Accounts* (New York: Oxford University Press, 2004); Robert C. Tucker, *The Soviet Political Mind: Stalinism and Post-Stalin Change* (New York: W. W. Norton, 1971); Milovan Djilas, *Conversations with Stalin* (New York: Harcourt Brace and Co., 1962); V.M. Molotov, "Address to Constituents, Election Meeting February, 1946," *Soviet News*, London, 1946; Francois Furet, *The Passing of an Illusion: The Idea of Communism in the Twentieth Century* (Chicago: University of Chicago Press, 1999); Isaac Deutscher, *Ironies of History* (New York: Oxford University Press, 1966); Jonathan Haslam, *Russia's Cold War: From the October Revolution to the Fall of the Wall* (New Haven, CT: Yale University Press, 2011); Frederick L. Schuman, *Soviet Politics at Home and Abroad* (New York: Alfred A. Knopf, 1947); Odd Arne Westad, *Reviewing the Cold War: Approaches, Interpretations, Theory* (Portland, OR: Frank Cass, 2000); John G. Whelan, *Soviet Diplomacy and Negotiating Behavior: The Emerging New Context for U.S. Diplomacy* (Boulder, CO: Westview Press, 1983); Deng Xiaoping, *Selected Works*, vols. 1–3 (Beijing: Foreign Languages Press, 1994); John R. Deane, "Negotiating on Military Assistance, 1943–45," *Negotiating with the Russians*, Raymond Dennett and Joseph E. Johnson, eds. (Boston: World Peace Foundation, 1951); Nathan Leites, *A Study of Bolshevism* (Glencoe, IL: Free Press Publishers, 1953); Albert L. Weeks, *The Other Side of Coexistence: An Analysis of Russian Foreign Policy* (New York: Pitman, 1970); Mikhail Heller and Aleksandr Nekrich, *Utopia and Power: The History of the Soviet Union from 1917 to the Present* (New York: Summit Books, 1986); Sarah Davies and James Harris, eds., *Stalin: A New History* (New York: Cambridge University Press, 2005); Robert Nisbet, *Roosevelt and Stalin: The Failed Courtship* (New York: Regnery Gateway, 1988); Marshall D. Shulman, *Stalin's Foreign Policy: Reappraisal* (Cambridge, MA: Harvard University Press, 1963) (N.B.: this author went so far as to allege that the Soviet-sponsored peace movement in Western countries in 1950s was evidence that Moscow sought peaceful relations with the capitalist West).

2. Cf. Deane's "Negotiating on Military Assistance, 1943–45" in Raymond Dennett and Joseph E. Johnson, *Negotiating with the Russians*; Deane, *The Strange Alliance: The Story of Our Efforts at Wartime Co-operation with Russia* (New York: Viking Press, 1946); Walter Bedell Smith, *My Three Years in Moscow* (Philadelphia: Lippincott, 1950).

3. Cf., e.g., Yevgeniy Anisimov, *Istoriya Rossii ot Riurika do Putina: Lyudi, sobytiya, daty* (*The History of Russia from Riurik to Putin: People, Events, and Dates*) (Moscow/St. Petersburg: Piter Press, 2008), pp. 471–2, 475–476.

4. For discussion of which see Albert L. Weeks, *Stalin's Other War: Soviet Grand Strategy, 1939–1941* (Rowman and Littlefield: Lanham, MD 2002), pp. 16, 18, 19–20.

5. See http://en.wikipedia.org/wiki/Stephen_E._Ambrose for a discussion of the errors he made in the scenario he helped write for the British television series *World at War*, narrated by Laurence Olivier.

6. Roberts, *Molotov: Stalin's Cold Warrior*, pp. 66, where Roberts also describes the Communist movement in Western countries as "socially-progressive patriotism"; pp. 67–75 and note p. 81, where he claims both Molotov and Stalin were committed to "tripartite collaboration after the war," that Molotov was a "realist," and later implies that U.S. obstructionism drove the Soviet leadership into a hostile posture. The same cause-and-effect is alleged by Mary Glantz, op. cit. and suggested by readings collected and edited by Odd Arne Westad and in writings by Leffler.

7. *The USSR: Institutions and People: A Brief Handbook for the Use of Officers of the Army of the United States* (Washington, DC: U.S. Government Printing Office, 1945). See analysis of and excerpts from this document in Appendix I entitled: "America's 'Democratic' Ally: What GIs Were Told About Stalin and Soviet Russia."

8. Cf. John Earl Haynes and Harvey Klehr, *Venona: Decoding Soviet Espionage in America* (New Haven, CT: Yale University Press, 1999), pp. 196–201, detailing Soviet agents' activities within OWI and the U.S. Department of State, and elsewhere within the U.S. government. Cf. Allen Weinstein and Alexander Vassiliev, *The Haunted Wood: Soviet Espionage in America–The Stalin Era* (New York: Random House, 1999), describing infiltration of U.S. Government offices by Soviet agents of influence, information derived from decrypted messages.

9. *Pravda*, February 10, 1946, p. 1.

10. *Pravda*, February 7, 1946, p. 1.

11. Djilas, *Conversations with Stalin*.

12. For a discussion of the downturn in U.S.-Soviet relations immediately after the war, see Albert L. Weeks, *The Other Side of Coexistence: An Analysis of Russian Foreign Policy*.

13. Cf. Haynes and Klehr, *Venona: Decoding Soviet Espionage in America*, pp. 215–216.

14. For discussion of which cf. Weeks, *Stalin's Other War*, pp. 16, 18, 19–20.

15. *Pravda*, February 7, 1946, p. 1.

16. Cf. Deane's "Negotiating on Military Assistance, 1943–45" in Raymond Dennett and Joseph E. Johnson, *Negotiating with the Russians*; Dean, *The Strange Alliance*; Walter Bedell Smith, *My Three Years in Moscow*.

17. Some revisionist-minded Cold War authors put quotation marks around the term, totalitarian, as if this "T-word" were merely a "hawkish" invention. Cf. Leffler *Origins of the Cold War: An International History*, p. 158. In his book on Molotov (p. 110), Roberts writes "free world" in demeaning quotation marks and with lower-case "f" and "w," in quotation marks as though that description were mythical. The revisionist attitude seems to reflect an absurd idea that might be expressed as follows: "By using such terms as 'totalitarianism,' 'Free World,' or 'Freedom Fighters, you are merely exacerbating presumed differences with the Soviets." Yet weren't such "differences" palpable and crucial? The current bias in this direction is again seen in "hawkish" reference to the People's Republic of China as "Communist China" let alone as "Red China." "Communist" and "Red" are considered by some media mavens today to be inflammatory, "cold-warish" epithets. They are rarely used by air and print media today. American teachers are known to be admonished for using them in the classroom. As though such terminology were a case of updated "McCarthyism" or "red-baiting." Incidentally, both Roberts and Leffler accept the theory that Stalin attempted to "appease Hitler" in late spring 1941. Yet, on the contrary, Stalin appeared to have been bluffing in this respect by seeking to put any blame on Hitler for any aggression against the USSR, since Stalin sought ultimate aid from the stronger West, above all the United States as he prepared for the inevitable worst. See Albert L. Weeks, *Assured Victory: How "Stalin the Great" Won the War But Lost the Peace*, Chapter 1, on this point. Too, both of these authors erroneously state that Stalin "collapsed" after the German invasion on June 22, 1941. This is plainly untrue and was merely part of Khrushchev's "deglorification campaign" against Stalin. Records of Kremlin meetings in late June

1941 show that Stalin was on hand daily except for a few days well *after* the invasion during which he was preparing in his dacha his amazing turnabout speech of July 3, 1941. These authors have succumbed to the distorted Khrushchev version of Stalin, which was skewed for political effect. Leffler does not read Russian so he apparently deferred to Roberts, whom he often quotes, for Russian source material. However, Roberts' selection of such material is biased.

18. Applebaum, op. cit., p. 22. The author cites official U.S. sources that show that such plans were discarded and were mere contingency projections of the type made by all major powers in their contingent security planning.

19. Applebaum, op. cit., p. 27.

20. Glantz, op. cit., pp. 19–21; 33–34 ff.

21. See http://www.oneparty.co.uk/compass/intercom/stalcom.html.

22. Prados, *How the Cold War Ended*, p. 184.

23. Albert L. Weeks, *Russia's Life-Saver: Lend-Lease Aid to the USSR in World War II*, Lanham, MD: Lexington Books, 2010.

24. Westad, op. cit.

25. Albert L. Weeks, *The Troubled Détente*, New York: New York University Press, 1976, Chapter 1, "Brezhnev's Ideology of Détente," where the facts are given concerning the USSR's largest military buildup in world history; the Kremlin's global-expansionist politico-military program; Admiral Gorshkov's building of a blue-water Soviet navy capability, Soviet positions of strength at geostrategic points around the world; its resource-interdiction policy, its first-strike nuclear strategy and violation of the "mutual assured destruction" (MAD) notion embodied in ABM treaty of 1972 that was violated by Moscow's deployment of offensive missiles in eastern Europe in the late 1970s prompting NATO response. Cf. pp. 20–33.

26. Albert Parry, *Terrorism from Robespierre to Arafat*, New York: Vanguard Press, 1976.

TWO
Cold War Basics

«Люди ссорятся потому, что не умеют спорить». ["Sides fall out with each other when they do not know how to cope with their differences."] — Russian saying.

"[In the first wartime meetings with Stalin,] Western negotiators were exposed to his tactic of abuse as a means of concealing his own weak position and his putting pressure on the other side. . . . Negotiations were often long and difficult [because of] Soviet feelings of insecurity, suspicion, secrecy, and xenophobia [showing] the futility of trying to build good will and expecting gratitude. . . . An essential element in the Soviet approach to the cold war was Stalin's ideological formulation of the 'two-camp' thesis." — *Soviet Diplomacy and Negotiating Behavior*, Congressional Research Service, Library of Congress (1979), p. 210.

"By Stalin's calculation as found in his unpublished statements (April 1945), Stalin claimed that within 15 to 20 years a new war would occur between the USSR and the capitalist countries." — A. I. Vdovin, *Istoriya SSSR: Ot Lenina do Gorbacheva* (*History of the USSR: From Lenin to Gorbachev*), Veche Publishers, Moscow, 2011, p. 264.

When World War II ended amid postwar appeals for no more wars of aggression, Stalin resumed his pursuit of ideological antagonism with the "bourgeois" West while laying plans for coerced annexations and violations of other nations' sovereignty. After 1945 Soviet territorial expansion resumed, as it had since the Bolshevik coup d'etat of November 1917. Stalin thus followed the dictates of Marxism-Leninism and his vow over Lenin's bier in January 1924 to spread Sovietism. Stalin remained absolutely wedded to ideological principles as articles of faith and guidance for his foreign policy. His writings from the 1920s to 1953 throughout his quarter-century reign show this ideological consistency.

His immediate postwar foreign policy was directly linked and affected by the principles of the official ideology. This appeared early on in various summits and conferences among the Big Three (the United States, USSR, and Britain) to which Stalin and his closest aides, like Vyacheslav Molotov, were parties. This rigidity was in evidence both during and after the war. It was as if Stalin picked up where he and Lenin had left off in "extending the boundaries of socialism" as Molotov called it. Historians on the USSR, including post-Soviet academic writers, describe how after the war, Stalin's traditional "brutal hand" at home was resumed in no uncertain terms. Only a few latter-day historians—in the West and in Russia—recognize Stalin's expansionist postwar foreign policy. Unabated were Stalinist hard-line positions taken by Soviet diplomats in meetings with British and U.S. envoys like Anthony Eden, Sir Stafford Cripps, John R. Dean, Averell Harriman, or even Harry Hopkins, close FDR aide whose admiration of Stalin seemed boundless. Deliberately finessed by the adept Soviet dictator in his personal encounters with such "Western bourgeois gentlemen" were Stalin's moods that were by turns amiable and angry (vodka would be poured for foreign guests while Stalin sipped largely alcohol-free Georgian wine and kept his wits).

Unmistakable signs of the makings of a future "East-West" struggle continually emerged even as the wartime alliance was in its wartime, fighting "anti-Fascist" phase. Ominous signs were already noticed by various perceptive Western participants in the first wartime high-level discussions that concerned opening a Second Front, Lend-Lease military equipment, postwar settlement, including territorial issues American participants in such meetings, like General John R. Deane, Charles F. ("Chip") Bohlen, Adm. William H. Standley, or George Kennan, perceived that the traditional, ideologically guided Stalinist prewar posture in foreign policy was still ascendant during and at the end of the war.

In other words, *seeds were planted for the development of a U.S.-Soviet Cold War* lasting from 1946–1991. At the same time, there is no doubt that the West, led by the United States, reacted strongly to the Soviet posture. We will assess how this reaction expressed itself and whether the oft-heard claim that dual blame for the outbreak of the Cold War rests on both sides more or less equally, has any merit as voiced by recent "revisionist" and quasi-revisionist authors.

During and immediately after the war, the populations of America and Britain may be said to have virtually fallen in love with Stalin and the bravery of Red Army soldiers. President Franklin D. Roosevelt but also the hard-nosed, anti-Bolshevik Churchill seemed charmed by "Uncle Joe." Examples of this could be canvassed under the rubrics of Cold War official personae as the source of one of the myths of the Cold War, or how outwardly friendly, personal contact and behavior at summits could mislead some of the participants, as Stalin regularly attempted to do vis-a-vis his Western counterparts, and most particularly Roosevelt. Such a discussion might be titled: the *unreliability of personal auras and impressions* as fragile bases for making judgments about adversarial leaders' strategy and intentions.

Widespread grassroots friendship for the Soviet Union was a leading Western motif in 1944–45. On the U.S. side, America's information service (Office of War Information) developed strong pro-Soviet views for the consumption of the U.S. Armed Forces. (Agents involved in penetrating and "influencing" OWI personnel at OWI is detailed in books about Venona.) Such domestic "orientation" reflected American public sentiment in favor of Stalin and the USSR. The American press in many cases was likewise misled by Soviet propaganda as reflected in OWI orientation and other sources of Soviet "soft power" influence (discussed later). Veteran Moscow correspondent Quentin Reynolds described the 1943 Hollywood film, *Mission to Moscow*, based on former U.S. Ambassador to Moscow, Joseph E. Davies' pro-Soviet book by the same title, as, he wrote, "a beautiful technical job [that portrays] a Russia that none of us had ever seen, This would have been all right except that the film purported to be factual and the Russia shown in the film had ax much relation to the Russia we know as Shangri-la would have to the real Tibet." "I wish Henry Wallace," Davies once wrote naively, "could come over and meet Stalin. I can imagine Wallace sitting down with Stalin and talking crops and arguing about when seeds should be planted. In his broad outlook, Stalin reminds me of Henry Wallace. Like Wallace, Stalin is immensely patriotic and, like him, he has a great love for the land."[1]

Under Stalin's leadership in the face of prewar Axis aggression, Soviet acquisition of geostrategic positions of strength—as a so-called "buffer zone" prior to June 1941—may have made some sense. However, at the end of the war following the four-year period of East-West collaboration, Soviet behavior was translated on the Soviet side into outright expansionism in violation of various Allied principles. This Soviet behavior jeopardized appeals, as stated in the Atlantic Charter of 1941 (to which the Soviets tacitly subscribed) as well as in the Declaration on Liberated Europe, adopted by the Big Three at Yalta, 1945, for respecting the sovereignties of other, smaller states, which Hitler had violated. . . . As Russian historian Yevgeniy Anisimov, a maverick historian, writes in his 2008 volume (see End Note 1 source citation).

> Communist influence throughout Europe became exceptionally strong. . . . Stalin was determined to carry out a policy of "sovietization," of setting up the Communist system in "old Europe" by legal means, that is, through "elections." In a new, more powerful way the USSR kept to its previous, prewar foreign policy of widening the zone of Soviet influence. The USSR made every effort to strengthen its influence in the Middle East. Northern Iran and Turkey also interested Sta-

lin as did the Bosporus and the Dardanelles. . . . The war had strengthened, not weakened the anti-democratic structure of the Soviet state. The totalitarian system, built up under Stalin, began to be extended to Eastern Europe in the form of the so-called "People's Democratic" regimes. All this could not help but bring about alienation of the USSR from its former Allies in the West. One of its leaders, W. Churchill, had said on June 22, 1941, that aid [Lend-Lease] would be extended to the Soviet Union regardless of the fact that the Prime Minister did not like Communism. After the war, Churchill again found it necessary to be truthful by stating on March 6, 1946, in his famous speech in Fulton, Missouri, that with the inception of the Cold War the end had come to the era of East-West cooperation. . . . With the Berlin crisis of 1949, the USSR, by means of a blockade, attempted to strangle West Berlin, which was occupied by the Allies.

The "buffer" territory seized by the Soviets to the west of its frontiers in 1940—deemed by Moscow, its fellow-travelers, and current historian-apologists and eulogists of Stalin to be territory legitimately seized in order to resist any future German attack—was *permanently* absorbed into the USSR. It remained so after 1945. During the war, Stalin had bluntly resisted Allied attempts to define the future status of these seized, formerly independent regions and nation-states and to reestablish their traditional, prewar independence.

These independent lands became sovietized as integral parts of an ever-expanding Soviet empire. The annexations became, in fact, one of the underlying causes of the Cold War break-up between East and West. With the Soviet Army's occupation of some half dozen countries of central, southeastern, eastern Europe and the Baltic region under Generalissimus/Gensek/Premier Stalin's dictatorial guidance, there thus began the phase of determined Soviet "satellitization" of these countries. (This eastern Europe is one of the world's oldest seats of civilization, more so than western Europe.) The whole world watched as these occupied, or "captive," nations (Austria was an exception when in 1954 after Stalin's death the Soviets withdrew their occupation forces from that largely agrarian country), which essentially remained oppressed nations. That is, until the demise of the USSR in 1991.

In the form of the Cold War, Stalin had thus unfurled, in Soviet terminology, another "anti-imperialist struggle," in Soviet terminology. With this aggressive, ideological policy came the establishment of the Cominform. The old Comintern had been dissolved ostentatiously by the Kremlin in 1943. This was an event that some optimistic observers took as symptomatic of a major Soviet shift away from Communist "internationalism." However, the Comintern's apparatus and its apparatchiks were merely transferred into the secret Communist Party Central Committee's Information Department. Both the Cominform and the Information Department served as surrogates of the old Comintern.

The ensuing Cold War should therefore be viewed as starting from the Soviet side at least by 1946. Lasting some forty-five years, it cost the two sides from $4–10 trillion each (the Soviets having spent the maximum). It was crossed with violent episodes and proxy wars that were encouraged and supplied by the Soviets and their newly-become quasi-ally, Maoist China. Besides the Korean and Vietnam Wars, over 100 other conflicts, as tabulated in the 1970s by the official Yugoslav Communist newspaper, *Borba* (Struggle) became part of the violent, post-World War II global landscape. All these wars and local conflicts, the Yugoslav Communist paper frankly acknowledged, were Marxist-Leninist inspired.

The Cold War mantra was reflected in the new world organization. In the United Nations Security Council after 1946, Stalin and the Soviet Union further displayed their postwar assertiveness and antagonism by issuing over 100 vetoes during the immediate five postwar years. This negativity helped isolate the USSR from the then other four permanent members of the Council: Nationalist China; France; Britain; and the United States. Stalin's militant blockade of Berlin in 1948 was simply one of several episodes in which the Soviet dictator single-handedly all but destroyed whatever remained of the comity that had existed during the height of East-West wartime alliance, which Stalin had touted in two addresses in 1941—in July and in November.

Needless to say, throughout the Cold War—indeed, from its very inception in 1946—Soviet media rattled with Cold War rhetoric. It was eventually returned with equal rancor and suspiciousness from the Western side. The Cold War thus became a deeply imbedded struggle in which, incidentally, many institutions and objective scholars in the West were personally attacked (this author included, as in a long *Izvestiya* article written by this government daily's Foreign Editor, M. Mikhailov in 1972). Better-known targets of Soviet media attacks included George F. Kennan, Prof. Frederick Barghoorn, Zbigniew Brzezinski, and other scholars. Insulting cartoons of American officials were daily fare in Soviet state-run print media.

More important, the Cold War saw repeatedly dangerous "brushes" at sea and in the air between armed forces units of the United States and USSR. In the Korean War, Soviet pilots secretly flew MiG fighter planes. Such encounters several times threatened to ignite a hot war, even World War III, between the two well-armed powers. The Cuban Missile Crisis of October 1962 during Khrushchev's reign was one such ominous event.

THE LOOMING COLD WAR: 1943–1946

A month *before* Winston Churchill's famous "iron curtain" speech at Fulton, Missouri, March 5, 1946, Stalin, on the preceding February 9, had already indicated that he had begun designing that curtain. It seemed that the Soviet dictator and his top aide, Molotov, were not satisfied with relishing the Allied victory over the enemy. They were turning their attention to strengthening Stalin's dictatorship and laying plans for further expansion of Soviet power abroad. Such expansion, including plans in the 1970s even for Soviet global hegemony, eventually went beyond territories immediately abutting the Soviet Union.

Too, soon after 1945, the same brutality that had accompanied his domestic rule before the war reappeared. Stalin's and Molotov's electoral speeches of early February sounded several ominous notes.[2] In Stalin's address, the Soviet leader declared that World War II had been no "accident." It had been, in fact, quite predictable. The war, he said, was not an ad hoc product of an adventurous Nazi leadership. It had not been caused by any "subjective" factors. In Stalin's view, the war had resulted endemically and necessarily from the capitalist system—that is, the system that still prevailed in the Western democracies after World War II.

In this ominous speech as well as in Vice Premier Molotov's for the same rigged election, the two top Soviet leaders proceeded to sketch out a postwar economic program in which, as before the war, heavy industry, linked to defense production, would be emphasized over lower, so-called "Group B" inputs and outputs of consumer goods. Moreover, the Soviet dictator appeared to be serious when he remarked to the Yugoslav Communist official, Milovan Djilas, in Moscow that same year that soon, as Stalin put it, "We'll have another go at it." He also told Djilas that the Soviets would impose their Communist system as far as the Soviet Army would reach.[3] Presumably, this meant another, eventual "big war"—World War III—a global conflict that, as Molotov said of the preceding big war in his interviews with Chuev in the 1980s, might further "extend socialism" worldwide. The Soviet Ambassador to the U.N., Yakov Malik, went so far in 1952 as to declare that "World War III has already begun" (*The New York Times*, Feb. 3, 1952, p. 1). Presumably, Malik's remarks reflected Stalin's thinking.

Throughout the whole postwar period, traditional Marxist-Leninist ideological pronouncements again and again cropped up in Soviet political literature. Kremlin-inspired vitriol about "capitalist imperialism" and the "capitalist encirclement" of the USSR again took center stage on the diplomatic level as well as in Soviet-controlled media. Meanwhile, Western newspapers still mostly emphasized the East-West wartime alliance. Yet under Stalin's direction, Soviet foreign policy clearly veered toward ever-increasing anti-West hostility.

The onset of a new, dangerous era of East-West tensions and outright armed conflicts—with Stalin's evident initiative—was a shock to all those in Russia or in the West who had entertained the notion of a new postwar live-and-let-live relationship between the Western democracies. Evaporating was their hope that a mutually agreeable relationship would prevail between the United States and the Soviet Union under Stalin's—

"Uncle Joe's"—leadership. Patent evidence, however, that Stalin and his Politburo colleagues were declaring a postwar Cold War, or "cold peace," with the capitalist states disillusioned people in the West. Still, in some cases, fellow-travelers—"*poputchiki*"—were unable or unwilling to impute the emerging hostility to Stalin's Kremlin. Such persons tended instead to blame Washington and the Truman Administration, which succeeded Roosevelt's in April 1945. Some contemporary revisionist and quasi-revisionist authors make the same accusation along with most—but notably not all—post-Soviet history textbooks published in the Russian Federation today (see chapter 6).

For some observers of non-revisionist and/or non-fellowtraveler persuasion, it seemed incomprehensible that Stalin would pick up the cudgels of "anti-imperialism," scorn capitalism and "liberal democracy," call the United States the "main enemy" in exactly the same way that traditional Soviet propaganda had always done before 1941. Added to Stalin's intractability and reactionism was the Kremlin's stepped-up, intrusive NKVD/GRU espionage against the United States during and after the war

As detailed in the Venona decrypts, this secret spying and influence-peddling in the United States were mainly directed at obtaining know-how for designing and manufacturing a Soviet A-bomb, but also at influencing American public opinion via sympathizers of the Soviet Union, whom Lenin once called "useful idiots." A prime target of a delay-team of Soviet agents, headed by Anatole Gorsky, was Secretary of Commerce, former Vice President, Henry Wallace. Having at first been duped by Soviet agents' overtures, Wallace later confessed:[4] "Many people have asked me how I reconcile my stand before Korea with my uncompromising anti-Communist attitude of the past two years. The answer is simple. Before 1949 I thought Russia really wanted and needed peace. After 1949, I became more and more disgusted with the Soviet methods and finally became convinced that the Politburo wanted the Cold War continued indefinitely, even at the peril of accidentally provoking a hot war."

The Soviet A-bomb espionage enterprise under Lavrenti Beria's supervision merged with Stalin's overall postwar defense plans—namely, to radically upgrade and modernize Soviet armed forces by adding nuclear weapons. In particular, this meant modernizing the Soviet Air Force, especially its long-range bombers, to give them ranges that would allow the bombers to reach targets in America and return to bases in the Soviet Union.

The Soviets also began research and development on rockets as carriers of nuclear warheads. The United States did not inherit all of Germany's Peenemunde rocket technicians and their know-how in designing and launching V-1 and V-2 rockets against England. In any case, the Soviets already had a leg up on the development of rockets. They were, in fact, ahead of the United States in that type of carrier of warheads. This advantage was proved all too obviously by the Soviets' Sputnik I achievement of October 1957 less than a decade after the Soviets' successful testing of an A-bomb and three years after their testing of an H-bomb.

In Cold War literature and Western press analyses, some observers recalled that tensions between Stalin and Washington—that is, between Stalin and FDR in the latter's final weeks before he died on April 12, 1945. Observers pointed out that tensions had alreadt begun to appear late in the war when FDR was alive. Earlier East-West differences had arisen over issues ranging from Soviet accusations (personally raised by Stalin in his correspondence with FDR) concerning delayed Allied opening of a Second Front in Europe. Stalin naturally opposed a Western "soft belly" invasion into the south Balkans—that is, into "his" bailiwick. Other Stalin contentions during the war and immediately after included these issues:

- The invasion's postponement until June 1944 (Operation Overlord) was attributed by Stalin, in his state-run media, and in correspondence with Allied leaders to Western stubbornness and/or as the Western Allies' deliberate attempt, as insinuated by Stalin, to deliberately see the Soviet Union bear the burden of war against Nazi Germany. Another omen of approaching East-West discord was Stalin's betrayal of East-West agreements concluded at the Big Three Yalta summit in 1944. These concerned promised establishment of free, democratic political systems in the countries of Eastern Europe under Soviet Army occupation. Moscow went about willfully violating the Yalta Declaration on the Liberation of Europe as well as the principles of the Atlantic Charter.
- Also antagonizing East-West relations during the war were Stalin's brazen accusations that the Western Powers would likely make a separate peace with Germany. Stalin accused his Western Allies of leaving the USSR out of the picture altogether as co-victor.
- Another Soviet propaganda ploy was to claim that the United States was planning outright to invade the USSR. An obbligato to this yarn, supplied by Soviet sources, concerned Hitler's death in spring 1945. The Soviet propaganda machine, with Stalin's approval, bandied it about that Hitler might still be alive, that he was hiding in the West and was about to reemerge to perform services for "Western imperialism." This tale reflected Stalin's game of firing off cold-warish accusations against the West.

Needless to say, these Stalin ploys were shocking to Western officials as well as to much of the general public in the West. Domestically in the Soviet Union, Stalin's rigid, hostile party line can be interpreted as a device to strengthen his postwar dictatorship by attributing evil intentions to the "capitalist encirclement" of the USSR, which would then have to increase its "vigilance." Here was the "external-threat" prop rationalizing the dictator's harsh policies. These included immediate postwar purges and the sentencing to the Gulag of Soviet POWs and refugees cruelly dispatched from the West back to the Soviet Union where they were punished.

As to the facts of Hitler's death, the truth was that Stalin's NKVD had recovered Hitler's remains near the Fuehrer's bunker in Berlin in May 1945. Soviet authorities well knew that Hitler had committed suicide. NKVD agents had several times, in fact, secretly moved Hitler's scorched remains in Berlin and vicinity to keep them out of sight. Certain anatomical parts, like Hitler's skull including his teeth, were sent to Moscow for examination, which confirmed they belonged to the Fuehrer. Today, Hitler's remains, including part of his bullet-riddled skull, are held under lock and key in the RF. That Stalin would resort to such hypocrisy in the name of advancing the Communist cause was both astounding and rueful.

These and other accusations and antagonisms emanating from the Kremlin were upsetting, of course, to most Western officials, and to the Western public. Soviet propaganda and behavior suggested a pattern of recurring tensions between East and West. The tension was likely to continue and even deepen, as it did, throughout the postwar period. In his famous "telegram" of 1946, Kennan spelled out what was causing this East-West clash. In the "Mr. X" article in *Foreign Affairs* in July 1947, Kennan observed:[5]

> There can never be on Moscow's side any sincere assumption of community of aims between the Soviet Union and powers which are regarded as capitalist. It must invariably be assumed in Moscow that the aims of the capitalist world are antagonistic to the Soviet regime and therefore to the interests of the peoples in controls. It the Soviet government occasionally sets its signature to documents which would indicate the contrary, this is to be regarded as a tactical maneuver permissible in dealing with the enemy (who is basically without honor) and should be taken in the spirit of *caveat emptor*. Basically, the antagonism remains. It is postulated. And from it flow many of the phenomena which we find disturbing in the Kremlin's conduct of foreign policy: the secretiveness, the lack of frankness, the duplicity, the wary suspiciousness, and the basic unfriendliness of purpose. These phenomena are there to stay for the foreseeable future.

Oddly, some contemporary authors on the Cold War still blame Kennan for the gist of his thoroughgoing, like the above, if rather pessimistic analysis. They do not put blame squarely on Stalin and his circle. For his part, Kennan had indicated how Soviet aggressive behavior might be "contained" by the West. Meantime, he wrote, some Americans will misinterpret spasms of purported Soviet cooperativeness. "When there is something the Russians want from us," he wrote in the same passage as the above, "one or the other these features of their policy may be thrust temporarily into the background; and when that happens there will always be Americans who will leap forward with gleeful announcements that 'the Russians have changed,' and some who will even try to take credit for having brought about such 'changes.' But we should not be misled by tactical maneuvers. These characteristics of Soviet policy, like the postulate from which they flow, are basic to the internal nature of Soviet power, and will be with us, whether in the foreground or the background until the internal nature of Soviet power is changed."

COLD WAR CALENDAR

The timing of the train of events and signs of this postwar East-West conflict are too often obscured in books about the period. The question of when and to whom to assign the initiation of the Cold War has often been addressed by Cold War writers and publicists. The issue was tackled, for example, in "Letters" in the liberal *New York Review of Books* of September 8 and October 20, 1966. The correspondence was published in response to controversial articles written separately for *NYRB* written by Arthur Schlesinger, Jr. and Gar Alperovitz. Both had debated as to which side, Western or Soviet, bore the responsibility for initiating the Cold War. For his part, Schlesinger had referred to French Communist leader Jacques Duclos's militant, "Cominternist" article published in April 1945 in *Cahiers du Communisme.* Schlesinger demonstrated to Alperovitz that the Cold War did *not* begin with Allen Dulles's falsely-alleged, "secret 1945 negotiations with the Nazis." Soviet-American Cold War antagonism, the famous historian wrote, clearly stemmed from actions undertaken by the Stalin regime, not by the United States.

This author commented in the *NYRB* in two published letters noted above that both historians were engaging in futile pinpointing of the exact start of the Cold War. I suggested that in any case Soviet-American animosity went back a good deal farther than April 1945, perhaps even as far back as the Bolshevik seizure of power in Russia in November 1917. Yet, if one were to single out an obvious, more recent event for the beginning of the Cold War, the Yalta Conference of February 1945—that is, a year before Stalin's and Molotov's militant electoral addresses of early 1946—might be a convincing starting point. This conference saw the first definite signs of a downhill course in Soviet-American relations.

As suggested above, the latest downturn in relations was the culmination of a process of East-West alienation that had set in during the Second World War itself. Early nuanced evidence of this was Stalin's decision in the mid-1940s to remove the moderate Earl Browder from leadership of the CPUSA (he was eventually expelled altogether from membership in the CPUSA). Browder was purged after French Communist Party official Duclos had attacked him in 1944. Significantly, in Browder's place the hard-lining William Z. Foster, on Stalin's orders, was made General Secretary of the CPUSA in 1945. It was an ominous sign of Stalin's emergent postwar policy particularly as it applied to America. Too, this indication came, notably, just at the time of Yalta. What transpired at Yalta, moreover, clearly demonstrated the beginning of the freeze in Soviet-American relations.

The details of this crucial conference in the Crimea of February 4–11, 1945, have been canvassed many times by assorted historians and observers. In this author's opinion, one of the best overall summaries of the origins of the Cold War and analysis of the Yalta summit may be found in *Soviet Diplomacy and Negotiating Behavior: Emerging New Context for U.S. Diplomacy*, vol. 1. This was a study prepared by a team of scholars for the House of Representatives Committee on Foreign Affairs in 1979 (see end note 1). The gist of the contents of this voluminous study was perhaps best summed up by George F. Kennan himself in his monumental, 8,000-word response to a U.S. State Department request in 1946 for an explanation of the then puzzling hostile Soviet behavior. Kennan's report was in turn summarized in his famous "Mr. X" article published in *Foreign Affairs*. Former U.S. Ambassador to the Soviet Union John R. Deane had described this behavior in similar terms in his book, *The Strange Alliance*, as follows:

> "In my opinion there can no longer be any doubt that that Soviet leadership has always been motivated by the belief that communism and capitalism cannot coexist. Nor is there any doubt in my mind that present-day Soviet leaders have determined upon a program pointed toward imposing communism on those countries under their control and, elsewhere, creating conditions favorable to the triumph of communism in the war against capitalism, which they consider to be inevitable."

The pent-up hostility between the United States and the USSR, shelved or obscured "for the duration," floated to the surface as soon as victory loomed on the horizon. As the defeat of Nazi Germany approached the whole postwar settlement of Europe clearly lay before these two most militarily powerful powers in the world, the United States and the USSR. Their bipolarity was thrown in relief by the weakness of both France and Britain by the end of the war. Of course, long before Yalta, Stalin and his associates had made it clear, and not only via pontifical ideological pronouncements, that the Soviets considered all of Eastern Europe to be their exclusive possession, a region to be "liberated" by the Red Army and subject to sovietization.

A rereading of Chapter XXXII of Robert E. Sherwood's *Roosevelt and Hopkins—An Intimate History* is instructive. In this chapter, entitled "Beginnings of Dissension," Sherwood, playwright and part-time historian, details the degree to which the Soviet-American "strange alliance" had deteriorated by the winter of 1944–45. Singling out the early period of

March 1945, Sherwood reported in his chapter on the Yalta Conference that by the middle of that month, a situation had developed in Rumania which strongly indicated that the Russians were determined to set up governments throughout Eastern Europe to conform with their own interpretation of the words "friendly" and "liberation." They would show little regard for the principles of the Atlantic Charter of 1941 to which Moscow had given at least verbal support. Moreover, Soviet machinations in Poland in 1944–1945 had also become a revealing sore point.

It was becoming evident, as Sherwood noted, that a complete deadlock had developed among the British, Russian, and American summit conferees. There was now a growing feeling of uneasiness among Western officials about the ominous aspects of the true relationship between the Soviet Union and the United States, Great Britain, and the other members of the United Nations. It was feared among some observers that a monstrous fraud had been perpetrated at Yalta, with Roosevelt and Churchill as Stalin's unwitting dupes. A similar description—and dating of Yalta as the manifest worsening of Soviet-American relations—may be found, for example, in Kennan's classic book, *Russia and the West Under Lenin and Stalin.*

The East-West freeze process had clearly accelerated toward the end of the European phase of World War II. While it is also clear that the Western Allies are not entirely blameless for the East-West disagreements that arose, it is clearer that Stalin's Russia played the crucial role in initiating what came to be called the Cold War. The Soviet leader did this mainly by supporting or instigating political, economic, and military aggression in the 1940s and 1950s.

Stalin's policy of Communist expansionism led to the formation of NATO and the Warsaw Pact Alliance, two armed fortresses facing each other. Stalin's rejection of the Marshall Plan in 1947 was especially symptomatic of the Soviet leader's postwar, anti-West posture. So was his promotion of a new ideological war that was outlined and led by the Communist Party of the Soviet Union by Stalin's favored Party Secretary of that immediate postwar era: the notorious, hard-lining, West-baiting Andrei A. Zhdanov, whose status in the Politburo had risen sharply by 1946.

A "New" Postwar Stalin?

During his maneuvering in the troubling, dangerous times of the late 1930s, Stalin showed himself to be a skillful if amoral leader. His speech of July 3, 1941, in which he touted an East-West "democratic alliance" (*demokraticheskiy soyuz*) against "Fascism" and for the "liberation of peoples" might have been considered a harbinger of imminent, positive change in the Soviet leader's overall attitude toward the West. Yet it was merely a pro tem call for East-West comity, an opportunistic posture pegged solely to enhancing Soviet weakness in the war and motivated by Kremlin appeals to receive Western Lend-Lease military aid. The latter had been offered by London and Washington even before the USSR was invaded by the Wehrmacht. This was a gesture that, of course appealed to Stalin whose country was not ready for a fight with war-hardened Germany.

Having "saved the Russian state," as some Russian historians today put it, the Soviet dictator after the war had the opportunity to show even more flexibility and statesmanship toward the West than was intimated in his watershed July 3 address just days after Hitler's invasion. Yet the Soviet leader refused to change his ways after the war. Why did Stalin deliberately sully the chance of his becoming the leader of a Communist authoritarian/totalitarian state who, as a leader would act as a postwar reformer at home while adopting a New Course abroad toward his wartime Allies? The "Fascist menace" had been liquidated by the alliance, or as the Soviets began to downgrade the alliance before war's end, "coalition" (*koalitsiya*). Yet instead of a New Course, Stalin restored his policies at home and abroad. He incorporated all the worst features of his dictatorship and methods of ruling the Party and state. These included the rejuvenated Lazarus of class struggle ideology; hatred of capitalism; and concern over the legitimacy of his own, one-party regime. Did Stalin resort to this reactionism because his sole motivation had always been merely to protect and increase his autocratic power? He had, after all, spoken occasionally of democracy and harmonious East-West relations in interviews and at the summits with the two other members of the Big Three. At home as well, Stalin could have carried forward the democratic-sounding promises made at the time of the 1936 "Stalin" Constitution. He could have realized the propaganda, paper promises that accompanied the constitution's appearance. However, instead of reform after 1945, Stalin became inflexible.

NOTES

1. Robert Nisbet, op. cit, p. 16ff.
2. *Pravda*, February 10, 1946, p. 1. This is the never-cited in Cold War literature electoral speech by Deputy Premier Vyacheslav Molotov, February 6. It carried the same ominous note as Stalin's electoral address (*Pravda*, February 7, 1946, p. 1). As explained later, Stalin claimed on the basis of Marxism-Leninism that World War II had stemmed from the "*second crisis of capitalism*," or its inevitable "aggressive" phase. This reference to inveterately embedded in Western capitalism as the prime case of war, including a future war, was regarded as ominous when it was reported in foreign coverage of Stalin's speech. No war, Stalin continued, "*can ever arise accidentally.*" The Soviet Communist system had saved the USSR and had liberated other countries he said: "The Soviet social order is better than any non-Soviet system in the world." The past war was won by Soviet "*active defense,*" suggesting that military preparedness was now a postwar necessity for the USSR. Without heavy industry, he said, Soviet defenses could not be built up: "To lag behind in emphasizing heavy industry means

to lose and bring about the destruction of the Soviet system. . . . [Such a buildup] will guarantee the safety of our country from any future contingencies." For his part, as noted earlier, Molotov, whom one of the Western revisionists praises for his alleged non-ideological realism noted that the postwar Five-Year Plan would result in the Soviets' "overtaking and surpassing economically the most highly-developed European capitalist countries as well as the United States of America. [This] will be accomplished in the nearest future." Soviet foreign policy, he said, will keep the *"aggressor pack chained. . . . This is why the Soviet Union is vigilant when it comes to possible centers of violating the peace and international security or to any intrigues along those lines. . . . The government and the leadership of the Soviet Army are doing everything to ensure that as regards the very latest types of armaments, our Army will not be inferior to that of any other country." Soviet participation in the United Nations "is aimed at preventing fresh wars and curbing all and every imperialist aggressor"* [emphases mine—ALW]. He boasted that the Soviet victory in the East had guaranteed that the USSR would be ranked "among the world powers. Important problems in international relations henceforth cannot be settled without the participation of the Soviet Union. . . . The participation of Comrade Stalin [in such affairs] is regarded as the best guarantee of a successful resolution of complicated international problems." He noted that the strategy used in the war "was under the immediate guidance of Comrade Stalin, our great Army leader."

3. Milovan Djilas, *Conversations with Stalin* (New York: Harcourt, Brace and World), 1963, p. 114

4. See http://delong.typepad.com/sdj/2013/02/henry-a-wallace-1952-on-the-ruthless-nature-of-communism-cold-war-era-god-that-failed-weblogging.html. See also Alex Ross, "Uncommon Man: The Strange Life of Henry Wallace, the New Deal Visionary," *The New Yorker*, October 14, 2013, pp. 107–108. In recent years, further revelations from the Venona decrypts show a pattern of attempts by Soviet agents to put blame for the Cold War on the Truman Administration. The contrast is made by such propaganda between Truman's alleged "warmongering" and FDR's "peace-making" where the Soviet Union was concerned. Cf. Allen Weinstein and Alexander Vassiliev, *The Haunted Wood: Soviet Espionage in America The Stalin Era* (New York: Random House, 1999). Via Google search, one may find examples of controversy over a 2012 documentary titled, "Untold History," by Oliver Stone, in which the writers make this contrast between the eras of Roosevelt and Truman.

5. Mr. X, [George F. Kennan] "The Sources of Soviet Conduct," *Foreign Affairs*, July 1949, p. 572.

THREE
The Myth of "Ideological Irrelevance"

Some Cold War writers relegate Soviet ideology to the status of ritualistic pontification. That ideology—a nation's creed and that of its leadership—could be taken seriously by a nation-state's ruling elite is unrealistic and absurd.[1] Quoting Donald Treadgold, Daniel Bell described ideological beliefs as a "false autonomy in the complex processes of decision-making in the real world."

Some Cold War authors, as do many contemporary Western Sovietologists, tend to agree with such views. They perhaps reflect agnostic Western attitudes toward political doctrines of any type. They subscribe to Bell's notion of the "end of ideology." A latter-day manifestation of this view is found in Francis Fukuyama's once popular book, *The End of History*. Another Cold War writer asserts: [2]

> Since ideologies supposedly adhere to ideological prescriptions in a monocausal and deterministic way, ideology must therefore dictate every action. [However] since there is abundant evidence ... that this is not the case, ideology is therefore not a credible way to view beliefs and their effects on actions.

The anti-ideology or "de-ideological" view is tantamount to alleging that, say, Stalin's program of collectivization of independent Soviet peasants or his extreme etatism had no ideological foundations. Soviet adoption of the Marxist-Leninist view of the inevitability of war as long as capitalism exists and the concept of "historical progress" as a deterministic process culminating inevitably in socialism and communism cannot be viewed apart from ideological axioms. These, together with other basic ideological bases for policy are supposed by some writers to be "worthless" rationalizations for the assertion of power by a self-perpetuating elite acting within a party-state. The role played by ideology as regime legitimizer certainly does apply. It is a natural marriage of ideas.

But this affinity by no means exhausts the influence of ideology upon foreign as well as domestic policy in totalitarian or authoritarian states. Some de-ideologizers further maintain that at most, Soviet Marxist-Leninism was mere sugar coating aimed at to assuring the public of the coming of a paradisiacal, utopian-communist future guaranteed by Communist Party rule. To paraphrase the Chinese proverb, as though "painting a cake satisfies hunger."

The skeptical Western view toward ideology held by certain authors recalls the old axiom, "We don't see things as they are but as *we* are." Western observers normally do not believe in the efficacy, or "determinism" of political ideologies and programs in their own polities.. Such writers regard them virtually as a form of American-Indian style wardance (Lewis Feuer had his opinion). Yet this widely-held view that ideology is no practical guide to politics—especially foreign policy—is clearly mistaken. As Anne Applebaum states:

> Across Eastern Europe, the Moscow Communists were united not only by a common ideology, but by a common commitment to the Commenter's long-term goal of worldwide revolution, followed by an international dictatorship of the proletariat. Though Stalin's declaration of 'Socialism in One Country' had brought to an end the open warfare between the Soviet Union and the nations of Western Europe, it did not prevent him and his secret services from plotting violent change. albeit using spies and sabotage instead of the Red Army. In the UK, Soviet agents recruited Guy Burgess, Kim Philby, Donald MacLean, Anthony Blunt and probably John Cairncross, the infamous 'Cambridge Five.' In the U.S. they recruited Alger Hiss, Harry Dexter White and Whittaker Chambers.[3]

Likewise, the notion of the "end of ideology" and its alleged irrelevance in modern policy making is fallacious. This is seen in the case of viable latter-day one-party, or party-state authoritarian or totalitarian regimes in the manner in which they make policy. A writer like the late political scientist, Samuel P. Huntington, developed in his classic *The Clash of Civilizations,* the idea that not only do ideologies matter, they become deeply engendered as "icons" or "cultural genes" within the several world civilizations. In a curious way, post-Soviet Russia under Vladimir Putin's rule embodies much of the mantra of former Soviet rule *sans* blatant ideological rationalization. Yet, his quasi-authoritarian regime in the Kremlin today bears resemblance to Soviet rule as though parts of the old Soviet ideology had "invaded the cell structure" of the contemporary Russian political order in ways that de-immunize the Russian polity from the persistent toxic elements of former Sovietism. The same observation can be made of Communist China today under the rule of Xi Jinping. His "fifth generation" regime and sets of policies embody much of the ideological fundaments if not all of the ad hoc maneuvers of the preceding

Maoist rule, 1949-to-1976. Don't the phenomena in both of these two nations testify to the virulence and influence of Communist ideology?

Moreover, to question the sincerity of a leadership's or an elite's commitment to a national creed is a non-starter. It is counterproductive in serious analysis of world affairs. De-ideologized analysis is even a potentially dangerous presumption. Some historians remind us of how observers and government policy makers once pooh-poohed Japan's Tanaka Plan of the 1930s. These creeds outlined Japanese militaristic-hegemonic dominance over East Asia. Or how Hitler's *Mein Kampf* was ridiculed and dismissed by some observers in the 1930s (Stalin, however, to his credit read the "Nazi bible" and took it most seriously). The fact is that these sets of ideological doctrines directly guided the policies of militaristic Japan and Nazi Germany before war after 1933. Marxism-Leninism did the same for Stalin and his successors throughout the Cold War up to 1991. In the USSR, ideology was an active, deterministic force. Which was particularly salient during the forty-year Cold War.

It is obviously necessary to appreciate the crucial role played by ideology in a Communist-ruled state. The leadership in the Kremlin, like that today in Zhongnanhai, the "Chinese Kremlin" in Beijing, earned its right to rule and make foreign and domestic policy from various hallowed axioms and phrases *handed down and drawn from the official ideology*. The whole of eastern Europe was sovietized on its basis. One of the most important of these was the notion that all post-Lenin leaders in the USSR were a part of the "Leninist Succession," as it was called, a kind of dynastic conception. Its equivalent in the PRC today is the "princeling" dynasty. For this reason, the sanctity of the Lenin Cult was itself absolutely indispensable to the one-party oligarchy. Leninism, Maoism and Dengism (from the thought of Deng Xiaoping) all play the same role in today's PRC as they would in many possible future cold war between the United States and the PRC. In China, such fundamental "thought" (*sixiang guan-li*, meaning "thought control") is their guiding ideological legacy. It is inscribed explicitly in the PRC Constitution itself.

IDEOLOGY AND THE COLD WAR

As noted above, in another sense, preservation of the ideology = preservation of the dictatorship. With reference to U.S.-Soviet relations and the Cold War, ideological protection of the one-party oligarchy in the USSR. was absolutely central to the party leadership under Stalin and his successors. Foreign relations were under its guidance. The unassailable purity of the ideology was naturally threatened by any adulteration by influence from American liberal democracy, as when U.S.-Soviet relations were in the news. Such adulteration would undercut the very rationale of the Soviet regime. The Soviet leadership, therefore, depicted the United

States, the most powerful liberal-democratic capitalist nation-state, as the world's most dangerous potential adversary of the USSR. It did this well before the era of the Cold War. From this it followed that U.S. capitalist imperialism was the most evil system in the world. According to Soviet ideology, the United States was Soviet Russia's natural "main enemy," to quote the perennial expression used in the Soviet political lexicon for the United States. Likewise, current Chinese military doctrine describes the United States as the "main enemy."

The Kremlin-perceived American threat to the Soviet's ideological system consisted of several elements.

First was the tremendous power of American media to carry the liberal-democratic "message" abroad.

Second was the widespread attention given American social, economic, and political developments in the foreign press of the world as well as the presentation of an often unfavorable contrast between the way of life in Communist states *versus* that in Western states.

Third came the intensity and persistence of what the Soviet press called the "American campaign of anti-Communism." Often this "campaign" was backed up, incidentally, by a higher degree of scholarship and knowledge of Soviet affairs than in any other non-Communist country in the world, as some foreign specialists conceded.

The fourth consequence of ideological "contamination" flows from the function of ideology as legitimizer of one-party dictatorship. This function consists of the basic concepts embedded within Communist ideology itself. The following is the rarely-quoted Stalin axiom about the legitimacy of one-party rule by a self-perpetuating elite, or the "most advanced elements" within the party:

Stalin wrote[4]

> Is it possible that the ruling [Communist] party immediately grasps the new processes arising and being created in life while at the same time being reflected in practical politics? I think this is impossible. This is not possible since first must come facts that are followed by their reflection in the consciousness [*soznaniye*] of the most advanced elements of the party. This means that only then can come the time when this consciousness of the new processes is attained by the minds of rank-and-file members of the party. Recall Hegel on this point: The Owl of Minerva flies only at night. In other words, consciousness lags to a degree behind the presence of facts.

Deng Xiaoping makes the same point in his *Selected Works*.[5] Namely, that it is the party leadership that possesses the necessary "science" to interpret the flux of events, facts, and processes. This supreme knowledge, or "consciousness," is possessed by the Politburo leaders is shared, first, with the party members (i.e., at party congresses, sessions of the

Central Committee, etc.). They then interpret it as they pass it on to the masses in simplified, understandable form.

The following Lenin quotation as concerns war (and consequently peace, as after World War II) illustrates the crucial role played by ideology in totalitarian or authoritarian states, and operated in the Soviet war against Germany and its allies, 1941–45:[6]

> If war is waged by the proletariat after it has conquered the bourgeoisie in its own country and is waged with the object of strengthening and extending socialism, such a war is legitimate and "holy."[7]

Lenin also taught that peace, as long as capitalism exists in the world, is only an interlude between wars.

Perennial disagreement among historians and also among some Soviet specialists revolves about the role played by ideology in Soviet policy-making, particularly as affects relations with foreign states. The argument is by no means academic. The dispute intersects with the main thrust of this book in understanding the anatomy of the Cold War.

Stalin's strategy on the eve of World War II raised the issue of importance to the origins of the Cold War, namely as to whether Soviet military policy was of an offencist/preemptive or of a purely defencist nature. Examining the underpinning for the making of Soviet defense policy, after all, must play a major role in deciding the question of the *postwar* Soviet posture, under the Stalin-Molotov leadership. For it concerns the regime's *doctrinal* views toward future wars—that is, whether between the USSR and capitalist states or between capitalist states in ways that ultimately involve the USSR. As, indeed, such an "intra-capitalist" war did and would involve the USSR according to Soviet ideology, with the onset of World War II in September 1939, which involved only some capitalist states. As Stalin predicted in the 1920s, this was to become a larger war, as incurred on June 22, 1941, that led in turn directly to Soviet involvement. Such discussion in the last analysis must bring about ideological interpretation as developed by all the regimes participating in such a general war.

A new Russian book on Soviet propaganda and ideology, especially as applied by the Stalin regime before and during World War II, is written by one of post-Soviet Russia's young historians. The volume makes this point about the ideological factor in Soviet policy making and military doctrine and strategy whether in peacetime, a cold war, or under conditions of war:

> In the 1930s and 1940s . . . the Bolshevik leadership confronted itself with formidable foreign policy tasks, in the solution of which propaganda was used as a virtual 'transmission belt' between the governmental authorities and the population.

Nevezhin, the Academy of Science historian cited above, also suggests that ideology guided Stalin in the making of defense policy as well as serving as a mirror reflecting the decisions that he made in directives intended for indoctrination. This was true of his policies that led to the Cold War. To imagine that Stalin had a problem "reconciling" traditional Soviet ideology with the Soviet alliance with capitalist powers is a fantasy that some Cold War authors like Melvyn and Geoffrey Roberts together with far-left writers, present to readers. For instance, Leffler states in his book, pretentiously titled *For the Soul of Mankind: The United States and the Soviet Union and the Cold War*:[8] "Stalin wrestled with the dilemma cursed with reconciling his concerns for security with his fears of capitalist encirclement, and the needs of the coalition with his obligations to the revolutionary project to which he had devoted his life." Poor, unfortunate Stalin and his so-called "dilemma," his "devotion" to his lifelong ideas! (See chapter 4 for a refutation of the ridiculous myth of Stalin's purely "defencist" security argument, which is clumsily worded in the preceding quote.)

The question of the role played by ideology in the matters under study in this book obviously must be addressed well ahead of the other factors determining the thrust of Soviet military doctrine and strategy in 1939–41 as well as its diplomatic strategy and tactics in that struggle. For if the direction taken by the Kremlin in its prewar relations with other states, not to mention its military doctrine, was guided by ideology, Marxism-Leninism then becomes as crucial as, say, Hitler's *chef d'oeuvre, Mein Kampf* or the Japanese pre-World War II "bible," the Tanaka Memorial (or "Tanaka Plan").

One may ask legitimately whether Lenin, Stalin and their cohorts and propagandists really mean what they often said about spreading communism and the Soviet system worldwide and using, as Stalin explicitly said, the "revolutionary base" of the USSR in order to subvert "capitalist imperialism" and "colonialism." Stalin: "The victory of socialism in one country is not a self-sufficient task. [It is] the groundwork for the world revolution." The Soviet Union is prepared, Stalin said quoting Lenin, "to come out even with armed force against the exploiting classes and their states." The Program of the Communist International put it (Sixth Congress, 1928): "The USSR . . . raises revolts [and] inevitably becomes the base of the world movement of all oppressed classes."[9]

Finally, this question arises: Was the forcible expansion of the borders of the young Soviet Republic immediately after 1918 and in the 1920s—into the borderlands of Ukraine, Byelorussia, Georgia, Armenia, Turkestan, etc.—really non-ideological, merely the reflexive, "nationalist" assertion of long-standing Russian territorial expansionism into neighboring lands that go back to the tsars?

On the other hand, if this Soviet borderland expansion coupled to attempts to sovietize the independent Baltic States as well as the more distant Hungary and Germany beginning in 1918, then was not the Soviet invasion of Poland in 1920, likewise inspired by the Soviet ideology of export of the Soviet "new order" (Lenin's term) as well as fomenting global revolution as propagated by the Third Communist International (Comintern/) established in 1919? If so, Marxist-Leninist doctrine must be viewed as crucially determinant in Moscow's casting of its "two-track" foreign policy. One track is Comintern-inspired expansionism, the other the pose of traditional diplomacy. It then seems obviously necessary to view much of Soviet behavior through the prism of the beliefs of the regime, that is, its ideology. This includes, of course, Soviet behavior in the immediate pre-World War II period as well as after the war.

As noted earlier, roughly two schools of thought have coalesced around two opposing views toward the role played by ideology in Soviet behavior. One school, consisting of the realists sees ideology in general as mere window-dressing. The so-called "traditionalists," on the other hand, assign a major role to ideology. Note: During his maneuvering in the, dangerous times of the late 1930s, Stalin showed himself to be a skillful, amoral leader who knew how to recognize the importance of ideology *as well as* how to flexibly maneuver within the ideology. It became what foreign observers called the dictator's "zigzagging."

Take Stalin's speech of July 3, 1941. This apparent turnabout and ideological shift in the address touted an East-West "democratic alliance" against "Fascism" and for the "liberation of peoples." Compared to the usual, boiler-plated renditions of Soviet official ideology, Stalin's speech just days after the German invasion of the USSR on June 22, 1941, could have been considered an ideological "reversal," a harbinger of imminent, positive change in the Soviet leader's overall attitude toward the West. Yet this was not the case at all.. Stalin's radio address was merely a pro tem call for East-West comity, a new posture. It was a tactical "retreat," to use the Leninist term. The maneuver was pegged solely to overcoming momentary Soviet weakness in the face of war. His speech was motivated by appeals to receive Western Lend-Lease military aid. The latter had been offered by London and Washington weeks before the USSR was invaded by the Wehrmacht. This joint London-Washington gesture appealed, of course, to Stalin, whose country was not ready for a fight with war-hardened Germany.

We must note that ideological manipulation is actually an *integral part of overall Marxist-Leninist ideology and of its suite of strategy and tactics*. In his now long-forgotten but germane *A Study of Bolshevism*, Nathan Leites described in detail the formula of Soviet Communist tactics (which is still copied in Communist-ruled countries). [Nathan Leites, *A Study of Bolshevism*, The Free Press, Glencoe, IL, 1953.] Leites brilliantly catalogued and analyzed such topics as "Retreat to Avoid Annihilation"; "From Retreat to Advance"; "From Agreement to Overt Conflict." In his discussion of such ideological positions, Leites showed how a virtual "Code of the

Politburo" was developed. He described what he called the "religious nature" of Communism. It is a creed, he wrote, in which "a limited number of terms and statements [compose] a specific language ... and code of action." In a sense, this set of strategy and tactics was a unique invention of twentieth-century totalitarianism. It is imitated by other authoritarian regimes. including those in today's world. Having "saved the Russian state," as some Russian historians today like to put it, the Soviet dictator after the war had the opportunity to show even more flexibility and statesmanship toward the West than intimated in his watershed July 3 address days after Hitler's invasion.

Yet the Soviet leader refused to change the basic tenets of Soviet ideology after the war. Why did Stalin deliberately sully the chance of his becoming the leader of a Communist authoritarian/totalitarian state who, as a "Progressive" leader would act as a postwar reformer at home while adopting a New Course abroad toward his wartime Allies? After all, the "Fascist menace" had been liquidated by the alliance, or as the Soviets began to downgrade the alliance before war's end, "coalition" (*koalatsiya*). As already noted, instead of a New Course, Stalin restored his prewar hard-line policies at home and abroad. He incorporated all the worst features of his dictatorship and methods of ruling the Party and state. These included the rejuvenated Lazarus of class struggle ideology applied at home and abroad; hatred of capitalism; hostility toward the West, and protective concern over the legitimacy of his own, one-party regime. Did Stalin resort to this reactionism because his sole motivation had always been merely to protect and increase his power? He had, after all, spoken occasionally, if disingenuously, of democracy and harmonious East-West relations in various atmospheric interviews with foreign journalists as well as at summits with the two other leaders of the Big Three. At home as well, Stalin could have carried forward—but did not—the democratic-sounding promises made at the time of the 1936 "Stalin" Constitution. He could have realized the much-touted propagandized, paper promises that accompanied the constitution's appearance in 1936. However, instead of reform after 1945, Stalin became inflexible and brutal. Can anyone believe that the Western powers were responsible for this, as some writers seem to suggest?

THE REALIST VIEW

In the dispute over traditionalism and realism, the latter, argues that ideology is mostly extravagant propaganda. At best, its function is to supply ballast and legitimation to a top-heavy, autocratic regime. Its legitimacy is questionable without the ideology that justifies its authoritarian, dictatorial rule. The absolutist regime's set of doctrines is foisted on the people and is to be followed to the letter. How else can the autocratic state be bound together top to bottom in realizing the party/elite's common cause, the practical goals of the regime? (Deng Xiaoping makes this point in his writings when he strongly criticizes Western liberal democracy's lack of centralized expeditiousness.)

Yet these dogmas and ideologies, it is alleged by the realist school, are impractical and visionary—in both the short and long term. To the realists, the political reality makes the dogmas all but irrelevant. Marxist-Leninist principles and goals are like songs sung to the choir.

For instance, consider the catchphrase for the much-touted millennial paradise of communism: "from each according to his abilities, to each according to his needs" and the anarchist-like dream in Communist ideology prophesying the ultimate, total withering-away of the state. These far-fetched axioms of Marxism-Leninism are viewed by many Western observers as so much sugar-coating, at best rationalizations in support of one-party rule. That anyone would actually believe such shibboleths, least of all, take them literally as "blueprints" for the future is about like saying that American Indians performing a rain-dance for tourists in New Mexico are to be taken seriously as though engaged in a serious effort to produce precipitation.

In short, to the realist school, Marxism-Leninism is little more than advertising, or boastful pontification. Realists could point out that in America clubs like Kiwanis, Rotarians, Masons, or chapters of a collegiate Sigma Chi Fraternity, likewise make vast boasts about their ideologies, millennial prognostications, etc. Does such posturing and mumbo-jumbo really mean anything? Above all, does it affect behavior in any concrete or significant way?

Moreover, in its ideological formulations respecting foreign states and their societies, Marxism-Leninism-Stalinism's dogmas, so the realists claim, likewise should not be taken seriously at any given time or place. Surely, these de-ideologizers claim, Lenin and Stalin and their cohorts could not have seriously entertained the idea of a future "Soviet of the Whole World" (Lenin's term that he repeated many times). The Soviet epigones may have *talked* that way to cajole or bemuse the workers, peasant and intellectuals or themselves. Or they sought to boost party morale and strut "militancy" for popular consumption. But that the leaders were actually planning and working to attain any such far-fetched goals, especially "world revolution," was and is regarded by realists as largely fatuous if not ludicrous. One can say that most authors, including some latter-day Soviet specialists, as well as Moscow (and Beijing) correspondents hew to this approach, at very least since the 1960s.

If the realists are right, then the many Soviet ideological pronouncements of an expansionist nature in the pre-World War II and Cold War periods can be taken with a grain of salt. In fact, they can be ignored altogether like some of the amusing episodes in Lubitsch's movie, "Ninotchka." Consequently, the skeptical view toward ideology invites a skeptical interpretation of, for example, the famous "Mr. X" essay by George F. Kennan, published in *Foreign Affairs* quarterly in June 1949. The views stated in that essay—in describing and analyzing Soviet ideology as a driving force of policy—were to underlie American and Western Cold War strategy for the coming four decades. Mr. X's views became boilerplated as the analytical springboard for formulating the American view of vigilant "containment" toward Marxism-Leninism and Soviet expansionism. It was a virtual subtext of the Cold War.

Even Kennan's earlier writings, for example, his "personal paper" drafted in Moscow in spring 1935, had a similar thrust. As he then wrote: "it is important to recall the fundamental peculiarity of Russian foreign relations. The masters in the Kremlin are revolutionary Communists . . . they themselves are leaders of the world proletariat. [The Russians can] tolerate ambiguities enough in practice but not in theory. *[Their] conception of foreign relations has had a profound effect, not only on the character of diplomatic life in Moscow, but also on the entire development of Russia's foreign relations.*"

Kennan's above observation that there can be "ambiguities in practice" ironically opens another realist front against the *traditionalist,* or ideological view: Namely, if ideology is so binding—for example, as with the Soviet anti-Fascist line in the Comintern in the 1930s—how was it that Stalin could conveniently discard this basic party line when he concluded his nonaggression, friendship, and trade pacts with the Nazis in late 1939 and 1940? Did he not suspend all anti-fascist points of view in Soviet media and official pronouncements for the short duration of enforcing these pacts? In this process, Stalin's Nazi-Soviet zigzag alienated many Communists and fellow-travelers worldwide. Ideology appeared to be have been put through the wringer. Put another way, fundamental Soviet national interests seemingly could cause strains in Moscow's official ideology. Which in turn suggests that ideology can be relegated to secondary importance in favor of other, larger *raison d'état* considerations in policy making in the presence of contingencies arising in ways that do not neatly fit into ideological frames. Such was the case, presumably, in August 1939 when the Soviet-Nazi friendship period was taking shape.

Yet the fact is that Communist credo, and "Code of the Politburo," leave room for zigzags and "tactical; retreats." These maneuvers are explained and illustrated with quotes from Communist sources as reproduced by Leites in his aforementioned works, *Operational Code of the Politburo* and *The Study of Bolshevism.* (See also Robert C. Tucker, *The Soviet Political Mind: Stalinism and Post-Stalin Change* for discussion of these Communist tactics and strategies that are so often ignored by conventional authors.) Such tactical maneuvers, it should be noted, still leave room for tactical *offensives* as Tucker notes:[10]

Communists can effectively work for peace [and] *intensify the cold war* [and] carry on the conflict against the imperialist enemy relentlessly ... redouble their efforts in the revolutionary struggle to wrest the world, area by area, out of the enemy's control and thus to destroy the imperialist system together with its accompaniment—war. [Tucker's emphases]

The above truism is totally absent in most writing about the Cold War.

Some authoritative Soviet military spokesmen, moreover, have insisted that *diplomacy*, not necessarily axiomatic ideology alone, can provide the best "preparatory," or favorable conditions for later waging of war. The same can apply to waging a cold war, as non-shooting war or cold war under the mantra of a non-shooting, "neither peace nor war." To wit, in his volume, *M. V. Frunze, Military Theoretician* (p. 381), Gen. Mahmud Gareyev, asserts: "Skillful diplomacy [*umelaya diplomatiya*] not only creates favorable conditions for waging war, but can lead to the creation of a totally new politico-military situation in which armed struggle can be conducted." Chinese Communist writings, incidentally, make the same point.

This well-known Russian military thinker thus suggests that through forceful diplomacy (e.g., in acquiring [annexing] Baltic and other territory in the 1940s), Stalin had prepared the USSR for waging war—whether defensive or offensive and whether or not the struggle were waged in peacetime or in war. Diplomacy in Soviet theory is a kind of "neither-peace-nor-war" (to use Trotsky's phrase) struggle.

Nevertheless, ideology, though playing an apparently subsidiary role at times, was still exploited as the principal rationalization for the sovietization of, for example, in Estonia, Latvia and Lithuania in 1940. The old "bourgeois order" in that region had to be overthrown; this was "historically inevitable." As Molotov said in his memoirs, Stalin succeeded in "extending the frontier of socialism."

In noting Stalin's relegation of Communist International (Comintern) interests to a lower priority with the shift in the party line on Nazi Germany, the realists seemingly make a good point. For by making his pact with the class devil in August 1939, Stalin surely was prioritizing what he considered at least to be Soviet short-term, putatively non-ideological national interests. He seemed to be placing the latter ahead of ideological principle. This, in turn, apparently made ideology, in the minds of realists, look irrelevant or expendable in certain crucial situations. As Soviet Chargé d'Affaires Georgi Astakhov reassured German Foreign Office State Secretary, Ernst Weiszäcker, May 30, 1939:[11]

> [Astakhov] explained how Russian relations with Italy. . . . as well as other countries could be normal and even very good, although in those countries communism was not favored at all. He strongly emphasized the possibility of a very clear distinction between maxims of domestic

policy on the one hand and orientation of foreign policy on the other hand.... The ideological barrier between Moscow and Berlin [Astakhov said] was in reality erected by us.

Likewise, after the German attack on the USSR in June 1941, Stalin again executed a zigzag that seemingly compromised the official ideology. He lost no time closing ranks with those same "encircling," capitalist-imperialist states of Britain and America, whom the Soviets from August 1939 to 1941 had singled out as the "main instigators of war" against the Soviets' anti-"plutocratic" friend, Nazi Germany. Yet by the next month of July, Stalin was addressing these capitalist democracies in the friendliest terms by dubbing them fellow "democratic," anti-fascist, war-"coalition" members. They were no longer characterized as "plutocratic" (the Nazi-like epithet used in both German and Soviet propaganda during the twenty-two months of the Nazi-Soviet "honeymoon"), or "imperialist" states, the terms used before late June 1941.

Forgotten, too, were those parallel "socialist" ideologies, Nazi and Soviet, that had prompted such statements in the German and Soviet press after August 1939, namely that the two systems had much in common. Still, the term "allies"—*soyuzniki*—was very seldom used by the Soviets to describe Stalin's new-found, "friendly," capitalist Western states that were later to make up the core of United Nations along with the USSR (*soyuzniki* was never used for German-Soviet ties during the "honeymoon"). When *soyuzniki* was used, it was applied solely to the Western Allies. Suspension of anti-Western, "anti-imperialist" ideology "for the duration" clearly had to be, and was made for the sake of the common East-West war effort. So that Stalin would continue to enjoy Allied support.

That this ideological compromise lasted only as long as did the war is grist for the opposing, traditionalist mill. As referenced by Kennan in his 1949 *Foreign Affairs* essay, Stalin and company never really renounced or revised basic Marxist-Leninist ideology. Their ideology, Kennan maintained, still imparted thrust and guidance to Soviet behavior in the international arena, both during and after the war.

Like the earlier Stalin promise made to the United States in 1933 to suspend Soviet-sponsored communist propaganda and subversion in the United States as the price for U.S. recognition of the Soviet Union, Soviet subversive activity, based on Marxist-Leninist principles and applied against the United States and other capitalist democracies, continued unabated in the postwar era. This was just as it had been just after U.S. recognition of Soviet Russia twelve years before. (In the heyday of the Nazi-Soviet honeymoon, the Germans complained of this Soviet perfidy, too, with respect to ubiquitous Soviet "active measures" and subversion in Germany.)

The following chart illustrates the dichotomy between democratic systems of government and the authoritarian (and totalitarian) systems. It is inserted here in the context of understanding the contrast between the two systems in the modern world.

Table 3.1.

Democratic	Authoritarian
Plurality of ideas, incl. pacifism, multi-party system	multi-party system war aims (*ad bellum*)
Separation of powers	Merged powers of government (executive; legislative; judicial) (*ad bellum*)
Obeying law about going to war (Constitution; War Powers Act)	Arbitrary going-to-war decision (*ad bellum*)
Free press and speech (opposition to on-going war); war propaganda ("Orientation")	Total control over propaganda and *Forcible* indoctrination of soldiers, civilians
Observance of Geneva Conventions	Arbitrary choice of weapons, tactics

THE TRADITIONALIST VIEW

The postwar milestones, among others, of this continued ideological, "internationalist" activity subsidized by Moscow were the famous Duclos Letter (*The Daily Worker* [USA], May 24, 1945) and Stalin's and Molotov's February 1946 electoral speeches. All of which signal reflected traditional Communist ideological notes. Churchill's "iron curtain" speech in June 1946 may be viewed *as a reaction to Stalin's postwar reassertion of the tenets of Marxism-Leninism and the expansionism "from the Stettin to the Balkans" and beyond that the ideology endorsed and inspired.* By the 1970s, some twenty-six countries worldwide could be considered active members of the Soviet bloc—that is, of the extended "socialist camp" of cooperative "client-states." All were committed to enforcing the principles of Soviet foreign policy and expansionistic "internationalism" in ways that conformed to the revolutionary principles of Marxism-Leninism.

As noted earlier, citing such postwar facts as the above, the so-called traditionalist school rebuts the realists' de-ideologization. Traditionalist scholars take seriously ideological pronouncements like *Mein Kampf*, the Japanese Tanaka Memorial, and, correspondingly, Marxist-Leninist ideology as formulated in the writings of Lenin and Stalin and their associates and successors. Traditionalists produce numerous quotations from the speeches and writings of Soviet leaders as they set out to prove their point about Soviet ideology as a practical, guiding set of principles, if not an actual blueprint of expansionism. Such writers dovetail Moscow's ideological formulations with actual Soviet policies. The writers demonstrate how the official ideology actually formed the basis for Soviet foreign policy.

In assessing the intent behind Soviet behavior on the foreign front, this school also emphasizes the practical importance of the global institution of the Third Communist International (Comintern) and after World War II, its successor, the Communist Information Bureau (Cominform), later incorporated into the party Central Committee's Information Department, Far from regarding Marxist-Leninist ideology and the Comintern/Cominform and other Soviet institutions, headquartered in Moscow, Warsaw, or Bucharest as mere window-dressing—traditionalist analysis considers denial of ideological influence by Western observers to stem from their being under the spell of the so-called "end of ideology" in their Western part of the world.

An exploration of the validity of the traditionalist point of view can start with an examination of the Mr. X (Kennan) analysis of 1947. If the Mr. X's presentation is convincing beyond reasonable doubt and Soviet ideology indeed functioned like the North Star to Kremlin policy making, then the argument that Stalin's et al., militant, "offences" ideological pronouncements on the eve of World War II and later during the Cold War would seem to have more than dubious validity. Ideological pronouncements thus become determinants of actual Soviet behavior toward Germany and its goals in World War II. They may even be seen to underlie the Nazi-Soviet agreements along with scuttling efforts at concluding collective security arrangements with the Western capitalist democracies. Do Soviet expansionist, ideological statements, then, prior to the German invasion on June 22, 1941, provide any clues of actual Soviet intentions and actions as respects the war's aftermath?

Several post-Soviet Russian writers refer to various militant ideological statements made by high Soviet officials in the months just before June 1941 (as well as during the Cold War). They claim that such statements could not have been made unless approved by Stalin. Furthermore, the statements themselves, they insist, above all reflect "offencist" military planning that must have been endorsed by the dictator. In peacetime such offencist took the form of aggressive diplomacy, For instance, in his essay in the Afanas'iev volume, *The Other War*, V. L. Doroshenko, noting the discovery by another writer, T.S. Bushuyev, of a new, revealing document, a speech by Stalin to a secret meeting of the Politburo on Aug. 19, 1939, writes:[12]

> Stalin needed the Second World War no less than Hitler. Stalin not only helped Hitler initiate it [in Poland], he entertained the same goal as did Hitler: seizure of power in Europe as well as the immediate aim of destroying Poland. Stalin calculated that the war, started by Germany, would lead to the downfall of the European order. Meantime, he would remain out of it for a time, entering the war at the most oppor-

tune moment. [Stalin's plans] were not only to conquer eastern Europe but to help bring about a communist revolution in France by going at very least as far as the English Channel.

War, as viewed by Stalin, suggested the writer, was the "midwife of the sovietization of the whole European Continent after the war." The Soviet side in Cold War reflected the same aggressiveness. The Politburo speech by Stalin makes all this explicit by stating "communist revolutions inevitably will break out" as the Soviet Army "liberates" Europe as a stage in the "development of world revolution."[13]

In M. I. Mel'tyukhov's contribution to the Afanas'iev volume, titled "Ideological Documents of May-June 1941," first published in the Russian military journal, *Otechestvennaya Istoriya* (No. 2, 1995), the author reproduces a number of statements made by high Soviet officials that he says amount to blueprints for waging offensive war in near future— meaning during World War II— in direct conformity with Marxist-Leninist "revolutionist principles." Statements are quoted from such officials as the No. 2 man to Stalin, Vyacheslav Molotov; party secretary Andrei Zhdanov; Aleksandr Shcherbakov, party secretary for ideology; and Soviet president, Mikhail Kalinin.[14]

Two such statements by the above illustrate Mel'tukhov's emphasis on ideology:[15]

> If you are Marxists, if you study the history of the party, then you understand that the basic concept of Marxist teaching is that under conditions of major conflicts within mankind, such conflicts provide maximum advantages to communism. (Kalinin, in a speech on May 20, 1941.)

> War will come at the same moment when communism is to be expanded ... Leninism teaches that the country of socialism [USSR] must exploit any favorably-developing situation. In which it becomes incumbent on the USSR to resort on its own initiative to offensive military actions against the capitalist encirclement with the aim of extending the front of socialism. (Shcherbakov, in a speech, June 5, 1941.)

> When conditions are favorable, we will extend the front of socialism further to the west. . . . For this purpose we possess the necessary instrument: The Red Army, which as early as January 1941 was given the title, "army-liberator." (Zhdanov's speech, May 15, 1941, to a conference of film "workers.")

The chief of political propaganda (PUR) of the Red Army, Lev Mekhlis, stated frankly at the 18th Communist Party Congress (March 1939), referring to the views of Stalin in a manner similar to Molotov and Zhdanov:[16]

> If a second imperialist war turns its cutting edge against the world's first socialist state, then it will be necessary for the Soviet Union to extend hostilities to the adversary's territory and fulfill [the USSR's] international responsibilities and increase the number of Soviet republics.

For Mr. X (Kennan), however, ideology was not everything. It did not cancel out other determiners of Soviet behavior. As he noted, "Soviet policy is highly flexible" and answers to real conditions beyond its borders, not exclusively to ideological dogmas. Moreover, he continued:

> The Kremlin is under no ideological compulsion to accomplish its purposes in a hurry. Like the Church, it is dealing in ideological concepts which are of long-term validity, and it can afford to be patient. It has no right to risk the existing achievements of the revolution for the sake of vain baubles of the future. The very teachings of Lenin himself require great caution and flexibility in the pursuit of communist purposes.... Thus, the Kremlin has no compunction about retreating in the face of superior force. And being under the compulsion of no timetable, it does not get panicky under the necessity for such retreat. Its political action is a fluid stream which moves constantly, wherever it is permitted to move, toward a given goal.

Translating the above and adding elements from the rest of his *Foreign Affairs* essay, we might conclude that for Mr. X—who in his monumental essay was surely reflecting on past Soviet behavior as well as what he anticipated for the coming years of Cold War—the Soviets may be guided or inspired by their ideology. Yet they will act cautiously, not "fanatically." They will not engage in reckless, offensive behavior but insert themselves only where a political vacuum appears. Their patience is "Oriental" (Kennan's term); they do not work against a rigid, world-revolutionary timetable. Applying the realist Kennan's views retrospectively, it would seem that Stalin would never risk war, as, in the Cold War, in the offencist sense of initiating hostilities out of the blue. He did not actively prepare for waging an offensive war against Germany or all of Europe in the 1940s, it is alleged. Nor did he think the USSR could expand itself by means of war after World War. At least, not in the short term. In a famous message to Belgrade in 1948, Stalin refused to be drawn into a war to seize Trieste for Communist Yugoslavia. Rather, as Soviet propaganda also stipulated, if war were forced upon Soviet Russia, Stalin would more than take up the cudgels and "extend socialism" abroad on the tips of bayonets. But only if attacked and "given the chance."

Stalin's hesitancy at first to go along with North Korea's, Kim Il Sung's, plan for the invasion of South Korea. When China indicated a willingness to join in this aggressive effort, Stalin decided to cooperate with the North Koreans and provided crucial aid and strategic military guidance to them during the war.

It follows that Stalin, if he was a pupil of the Chinese strategist Sun Tzu, would agree that the best victory was one that was obtained by a minimum of armed fighting, or even by none at all. "Weapons are ominous tools," Sun Tzu wrote, "to be used only when there is no other alternative" to satisfy a state's ambitions.

Could it also be that the Soviets' massive, ongoing military buildup in 1939–41, and later through the 1970s accompanied as it was by threatening tones of militancy in its propaganda, were aimed mainly at scaring off any likely aggressor rather than in preparation for unilaterally initiating war? Was Stalin and his successors so cautious that they were not about to risk what Kennan called destruction of all the achievements of the Soviet Union—its factories and cities, and the Communist one-party rule and superstructure—in risky, untimely war-making? As Stalin proclaimed in 1925:[17]

> If war is to break out, we won't be able to stand by idly. We will have to enter the fray but we will be the last ones to do it in order to the decisive weight on the scales, a weight that must tip the balance.

Stalin had another tactic in mind—an ideological subplot, as it were—that both he and Lenin had often mentioned in the context of war-as-midwife-revolution. That was *encouragement of intra-imperialist discord*. This tactic was partly ideological and partly diplomatic and military. It appeared during the Cold War as assertion of Stalin's newfound hubris as the leader of the postwar superpower. All major decisions in global politics, the Soviets boasted, would from now on include the power of the USSR.

SOVIET DIPLOMATIC "WARFARE"

A key element of Soviet diplomatic strategy and tactics in the Kremlin's waging of the Cold War was a set of formulae that governed Soviet diplomatic behavior. The USSR Ministry of Foreign Affairs was an institution designed to carry out not only conventional diplomatic tasks. Its function was mainly to realize strategic ideological goals. This was and in some respects still is seen in today's post-Soviet diplomatic "struggle" with the following Russian aims and methods:[18]

- To win "political territory" in any disputes with adversaries. Soviet and post-Soviet foreign policy is not designed to compromise in significant ways or to serve win-win situations. It is designed to achieve tangible victories (see General Gureyev's statement, above).
- A standby of Soviet postwar as well as post-Soviet diplomatic tactics is to exploit delay in order to achieve ultimate diplomatic victory.

- The "two incompatibles" in Soviet foreign policy—the disruptive spirit and goals of ideology *versus* the professionalism of diplomacy—were inevitably resolved in favor of basic Soviet strategic ideological goals. For instance, use of delaying tactics with Soviet signing of documents that promised uninhibited liberation and protection of nations' sovereignty combined with vague promises about the "democratic" future of postwar eastern Europe (Poland's fate being one of the most salient) showed how diplomatic niceties merely served ideological ends and were subordinated to basic Soviet goals that satisfied Marxist-Leninist revolutionism.
- Exploitation of diplomacy to serve long-range Soviet strategy of winning favor abroad for the USSR. Under Stalin and his successor, the Soviets were infamous in offering all sorts of appealing policy initiatives which, however, were never realized, nor were they ever intended to be realized. Such posturing became show-case *"pokazukha"*—(i.e., done for show) to enhance Soviet prestige and its "public face" worldwide. Events such as the Treaty of Rapallo of 1922, Soviet acceptance of U.S. requirements for American recognition of the USSR (1933), vast Soviet proposals for atomic and arms controls (e.g., like the 1972 ban on types of anti-missile defense that Moscow proceeded secretly to violate); Soviet backed peace movements aimed at weakening the West; Soviet support of the Atlantic Charter and the Declaration on the Liberation of Europe as the Kremlin planned measures that countered the spirit of such agreements.[19]

NOTES

1. James A Dougherty and Robert L. Pfaltzgraff,Jr., *Contending Theories of International Relations*, second ed (New York: Harper and Row, 1981), p. 114. The authors write: "Like [Hans] Morgenthau, [Henry] Kissinger views with disfavor the injection of ideology into the international system." It might be added, they also object to its introduction into the discussion of how nation-states make their foreign policy. This view, in my opinion, is mistaken, and yet is a popular standby in the view of those several Cold War authors who regard themselves as "Realists" et al., on the Cold War op. cit.) insert this dagger (vol. 2, pp. 522–3: "professional Cold Warriors, blinded by their ideological bent, refused to admit [that the USSR and the United States could ever cooperate]." Perhaps such people as Byrnes, Kennan, Weinberger, or Gates thought in that negative way was because of the seventy-five-year-plus record of Soviet expansionism! Yet it was President Reagan who had once used the term "evil empire" to describe the Soviet Union, who was able to strike a bargain on arms with Soviet leader Mikhail Gorbachev despite his writings in the 1970s in which traditional ideology was uppermost. Analysts obviously had to analyze all of Gorbachev's writings prior to his meetings with Reagan after 1983. Yet in vol. 1 of Graebner et al.'s book, the authors, or some part of them (there are four altogether), give due emphasis to ideological underpinning for the aggressive policies of Stalin and his successors up to 1991. In other words, the quadruple authors' book on the Cold War includes numerous contradictions, possibly stemming from the multiple authors involved in the writ-

ing. Graebner himself had written a good deal in his published articles during the Cold War about the threatening aspect of Soviet ideology. One gets the impression the other writers on the team disagreed with him thus giving the book the quality of a four-headed monster.

2. Odd Arne Westad, *Reviewing the Cold War: Approaches, Interpretations, Theory* (New York: Frank Cass, 2006), p. 186.

3. Applebaum, op. cit., p. 53.

4. J. V. Stalin, *Sochineniye*, (Gosizdat: Moscow, 1949), vol. 5, p. 232, from a Stalin writing dated May 31, 1930. This extremely significant, revealing statement by Stalin is persistently ignored in most Western literature on Marxism-Leninism-Stalinism. Yet its postulates lie at the very foundation of any totalitarian/authoritarian system.Nor has today's China with its "enrich yourself," state-capitalism program ignored Marxist teaching.

Latter-day Chinese Communist Marxism, as it turns out, is an orthodox form of the dogma.

Some observers in the West mistakenly claim that China has forgotten Marxist teaching altogether. The PRC, they say, has adopted fullfledged capitalism. Yet far from regarding Marx as an antique of the 19th century or a form of routine positivism, the ideology of Mao's successors, Deng Xiaoping and the three generations of Party leaders since 1978, are clearly orthodox Marxists. Nikolai Bukharin's (1888–1938) axiom for Russian capitalists was "enrich yourselves" in the Soviet Union of the 1920s. This is the line of Deng Xiaoping. and his followers. Deng himself became personally acquainted with Bukharin's theories when he resided in the Soviet Union for a year in the mid-1920s after being expelled from France.

Today's Chinese interpreters of Marx, who keep Marxism relevant in the twenty-first century just as they do Marxist theory of one-party dictatorship, make the following, seemingly valid point: For a country to realize socialism let alone attain fullfledged communism ("to each according to his need"), no cretinized "iron bowl" of economic backwardness as per Mao's misguided "Great Leap Forward" from 1958–1961 (which anti-capitalist policy Mao came to regret) is truly Marxist. Bukharin and others, whose writings were absorbed by ideologically-oriented Chinese officials like Deng—namely, Zhao Ziyang, Liu Shaoqi, and others—were consistent Marxists. Following the logic of dialectical materialism, they advocated *a protracted capitalist phase in order to attain economically-abundant socialism*. Indeed, Chinese ideologists currently say that this process could take "100 years."

In his early days, Mao himself advocated support of petty-bourgeois industry as a necessary, preparatory economic stage for China (under, of course, the "people's democratic dictatorship") leading to socialism. This process would be guided within a political system dominated by the Chinese Communist Party. This phase Lenin had always admitted. In his seminal writings of 1905 as well as in his support of "state capitalism" under the New Economic Policy (NEP) after 1921, Lenin asserted that the phase of capitalist development would duly progress to socialism. Yet this must take place under the strict leadership and guidance of the party "vanguard." This fully conformed to the idea of the *Communist Manifesto* concerning dictatorial rule by those who singly "understand the line of march," as Marx and Engels phrased it—viz., the enlightened leadership of the Communist Party

The notion of necessary dialectical completion of the capitalist phase was largely Bukharin's during the NEP (New Economic Policy) of the 1920s. This was the view later adopted by Deng Xiaoping. As "paramount leader" in Zhongnanhai (the "Chinese Kremlin") by the late 1970s, Deng finally had the power to apply Buharinism to China and thus complete the necessary capitalist phase as guided by the Party. In the Chinese view, calling this capitalist phase "socialist" is no contradiction. It is firmly based on Marxist as well as Leninist texts.

Two conclusions emerge from the above.

First, as far as China is concerned, Marx is by no means "dead" nor has it been consigned to the dustbin of antiquated nineteenth-century philosophy. Second, the

Marxist tradition is especially alive and well in China. To quote Hu Jintao's and Xi Jinping's propaganda line, the Marxian idea of enlightened, "scientific" dictatorship is being applied full time in the PRC. As to rehashing the final "fully-communist phase" as projected by Marxist writings (e.g., in the Marx-Engels' *German Ideology*, the Chinese realistically, as well as shrewdly, leave that ultimate phase largely unaddressed and undescribed. They merely assert that any such distribution of economic wealth on a fully communist basis is obviously impossible until the Chinese economy is producing the material basis for society's economic abundance and equality. Chinese ideologists assert that this could take as long as a century, Obviously, they do not wish to indulge in extravagant predictions. They want to avoid piling up, as they say of the CPSU under Khrushchev, Brezhnev et al., unfulfilled, self-defeating, utopian promises. Which they scorn in their Party literature as "Khrushchevism."

5. Deng Xiaoping, *Selected Works: 1975–1982* (Beijing: Foreign Languages Press, 1984), pp. 320–321.

6. V. A. Nevezhin, *Sindrom nastupatel'noi voiny* (Syndrome of Offensive War) (Moscow: Airo-XX, 2000), pp. 252–253. David Glantz's otherwise two excellent studies of Soviet combat in the Great Patriotic War (see Bibliography)—in his referencing of Soviet weapons and tactics and strategy—not a word is devoted to Marxist-Leninist ideology. Yet concerted indoctrination of Red Army servicemen in those principles was aimed at making them better soldiers. It is obvious that commanders, up to and including the commander-in-chief, Stalin, likewise were guided by the principles of the official doctrine. That ideology and instilling morale and a sense of purpose in soldiers—and civilians in the postwar period—are one and the same. This function of ideology was first proposed by Napoleon. In ancient times as well parallels may be found (e.g., Pericles' propagandistic Funeral Oration extolling Athens). The point about the perennial uses of ideology in preparation for and waging war is strongly asserted. It is no less important under conditions of postwar "struggles." In all editions of the *Soviet Military Encyclopedia*, including an article titled "Mythology," ideology is accorded a major role. In his *Collapse of the Grand Alliance 1945–1948*, James M. Gormly makes no mention at all of Marxism-Leninism or ideological motivations for Soviet behavior. In one place where he mentions Lenin, Gormly uses the odd, meaningless expression "Leninist isolationism" (p. 87). If Lenin favored isolationism, why did he establish in 1919 what he called the Moscow-based "General Staff of World Revolution"?

7. V. I. Lenin, *Selected Works* (New York: International Publishers, 1943), vol. 7, p. 357. For many other similar statements by Lenin, Stalin and other high Soviet officials, see Albert L. Weeks, *Soviet and Communist Quotations* (Washington, DC: Pergamon-Brassey's), Chapter 16.

8. Leffler, *For the Soul of Mankind*, p. 72. Dependable Cold War author, Jonathan Haslam, op. cit., describes one of the Cold War writers as an ideological "staunch leftist." Haslam, op. cit. p. 303. A "clash of ideologies," in other words. It may be true that current Cold War revisionism is a leftist deviation.

9. Weeks, op. cit., pp. 246–7.

10. Robert C. Tucker, *The Soviet Political Mind: Stalinism and Post-Stalin Change* (New York: W. W. Norton, 1971).

11. Jiri Hochman, *The Soviet Union and the Failure of Collective Security, 1934–1938*, (Ithaca, NY: Cornell University Press, 1984), pp. 176–7.

12. Albert L. Weeks, *Stalin's Other War: Soviet Grand Strategy, 1939–1941* (Lanham, MD: Rowman and Littlefield, 2002), p. 17.

13. Ibid., p. 20.

14. Yuri N. Afanas'iev, *The Other War* (Moscow: Rossiiskii Gosudarstvenniy Universitet, 1996), pp. 60-75. The full text of Stalin's speech is reproduced in this section and in Weeks, *Stalin's Other War*, Appendix.

15. Ibid., pp. 95, 97.

16. M. I. Semiryaga, "*Sovetskiy Soyuz I vneshnyaya politika SSSR,*" *Voprosy istorii*, No. 9, 1990, p. 61. Semiryaga is a respected doctor of historical sciences, State Prize laureate

(USSR), and today a scholar in the Russian Academy of Sciences. A prolific researcher and writer, Dr. Semiryaga inclines toward the "offencist" school in interpreting Stalin's policies and actions before June 1941. He is one of the contributors to the Afanas'iev volume cited above.

17. Helpful in defining this discussion are the following, among many others: Joseph G. Whelan, *Soviet Diplomacy and Negotiating Behavior: The Emerging New Context for U.S. Diplomacy* (Boulder, CO: Westview Press, 1983); John N. Hazard, *The Soviet System of Government* (Chicago: University of Chicago Press, 1964); Raymond Dennett, Joseph E. Johnson, eds., *Negotiating with the Russians* (Boston: World Peace Foundation, 1951); William H. Standley, *Admiral Ambassador to Russia* (New York: Henry Regnery Company, 1955); James F. Byrnes, *Speaking Frankly* (Westport, CT: Greenwood Press, 1947); Charles Bohlen., *Witness to History, 1929–69* (New York: W.W. Norton, 1973); George F. Kennan, *Soviet Foreign Policy, 1917–1941* (Princeton, NJ: Van Nostrand, 1960).

18. Stalin adroitly "touched" on various issues in ostensibly "cooperative" ways during the East-West summits by way of delaying resolution of said issues. For instance, in informal conversations laced with smiles, food, and drink, a smiling Stalin indicated support of Western values of democracy and respect for national sovereignty while delaying actual instrumentation of agreements that would fulfill the promises. In this way, Stalin could proceed systematically to sovietize the Baltic and east European region while the Western Allies only complained and did nothing tangible to block the Soviets. With the result that the Soviet occupation of the whole region took the form of outright expansionism (as promised by Zhdanov) expansionism and boasted of by Molotov in his memoirs. This was in gross violation of previous vague promises, by the Soviet leader not to mention formal documents.

19. Such a dichotomy—and consequent duplicity—is the result of the well-known "two track" nature of Soviet diplomacy by which a conventional front is out to mislead adversaries as to basic Soviet, ideological-driven strategy.

FOUR
Fallacy of Stalin's "Defencist" Security

When President Putin lamented the demise of the USSR as the "greatest catastrophe of the twentieth century,"[1] he was not suffering from nostalgia over the loss of the Communist system. His quasi-authoritarian rule today, which resembles that of Napoleon III, bears little resemblance to the Marxist-Leninist dictatorship in Russia 1917 to 1991. In his lament, Putin, above all, was expressing the significance of the loss of the resource-rich as well as geostrategic territory that was once under Soviet imperial sway in European Russia as well as in Central Asia and the Far East.

Following World War II with the Soviet Army occupying all of Eastern Europe, Stalin, an aggressive player in the Big Three wartime alliance, had no intention of losing imperial control over the new territory west of Russia proper that was illegally incorporated into the USSR under the Stalin-Molotov pact with Nazi Germany in 1939. These Nazi-Soviet deals included Soviet seizure of half of Poland and parts of other non-Russian territory in late 1939 and in 1940 (see discussion of Soviet expansion below).

STALIN'S EMPTY ARGUMENT

Stalin's intention to retain control of these seized foreign territories was made clear by the Soviet dictator early on in 1942 in his pregnant talks with British Foreign Secretary Anthony Eden in Moscow in summer 1941. To call Stalin's postwar territorial demands for imperial rule over the three independent Baltic nations and those of eastern and central Europe as "defencist" and fully justifiable, as some Cold War authors suggest, is inexcusable. Sovereign states, like Estonia or Poland, the largest east European country, that were fully sovietized before and after World War II during the Cold War, were hardly themselves ever a "threat" to the giant Soviet Russia. Although this claim was made by Stalin and Soviet propaganda and by some Western apologists for Soviet behavior, like Joseph E. Davies, Henry Wallace, and a number of Cold War writers. Only the larger, powerful countries, like Nazi Germany in World War II or the Central Powers led by Germany in World War I, forced these small nations to fall under the sway of the bigger aggressor countries that dominated them. The latter became pawns and part of the larger tangible threat to Russian security represented by the major powers. It was the controlling "back pieces" on the chessboard that ordered the pawns of central and eastern Europe to obey and become hostile toward Russia. It is not surprising that elements within such countries could be found who welcomed cooperation with these aggressor powers. For one thing, such elements feared Soviet expansionism, and for good reason. Their independence had continuously been mauled and threatened by their big Communist neighbor since 1918, a power whose ideology explicitly called for Soviet-led subversion of such "bourgeois" nation-states.

Stalin once plaintively mentioned to Churchill that Eastern Europe had acted "three times" in history, he said, as a "springboard" for invasions of Russia. He presumably meant invasions in the Napoleonic wars of the early nineteenth century, World War I, and the Nazi invasion of June 1941. Yet France, too, had suffered multiple historic invasions—three, in fact, in the nineteenth and twentieth centuries, but France did not claim that that entitled the French to "occupy" and "frankify" the Netherlands, Belgium, Luxemburg, Switzerland, or Italy, which border on France (the Ruhr after World I was a minor exception when France and Belgium occupied it, but then returned it to Germany in the mid-1920s).

For Stalin in 1940-to-1948, to have reserved the right to sovietize these small nations and all but making them integral SSR republics of the Soviet empire was simply unacceptable by International Law and practice. Accordingly, the United States never recognized these Soviet annexations. Washington always insisted that most of these territories bordering Soviet Russia—having become independent, sovereign states after World War I—were entitled to their independence. Yevgeniy Anisimov notes that:

> At Yalta [Feb. 5, 1945] Stalin succeeded in blocking attempts by the [Western] Allies to thwart his control over Poland. In this way, the Allies perforce recognized the existence of the Soviet empire [*sovetskoi imperii*], the surrounding "sphere of Soviet influence,' and the satellitization of these countries.[2]

In the first year of Bolshevik rule in Russia, the Lenin regime ostentatiously formally recognized their independence. Only later did the Lenin and Stalin regime violate this promise beginning with the sovietization of

Ukraine in 1919 and attempted sovietization of other bordering nations. During World War II, U.S. officials demanded via the Atlantic Charter, the Declaration of the Liberation of Europe, and other documents with the force of international law that all countries victimized by aggression have their national sovereign rights returned to them. Needless to say, emigre representatives of said victimized, captive nations never gave up their efforts to regain their countries' national independence—in this case, from the USSR.

MOSCOW'S POST-SOVIET ATTEMPTS AT UNITY

In the current post-Soviet period during his three presidential terms, Putin has been angling to restore unity centered on Moscow vis-à-vis the former republics of the Soviet Union. Their populations—or "human capital," as Stalin called it—once composed nearly half that of the Soviet Union as a whole. Restoration of any such unit would necessarily become some form of renewed Kremlin control from the center to whatever degree. At least this appears to be Putin et al.'s intention. Note that Russia proper itself was once geographically synonymous with the former Russian Soviet Federated Socialist Republic (RSFSR). The latter by its multiple time-zone size was politically dominant over the other, smaller republics. Two-thirds of the RSFSR, like the post-Soviet Russian Federation today, lay in Siberia, or east of the Urals.

Today these fully-independent, non-Russian, ex-republics to the east and to the west are separate, sovereign nation-states. The richest ones lie in the southern, Central Asian part of the former USSR abutting Mongolia and China. They were once part of the ancient Silk Road leading from China-ruled territory to the Western world, a "road" China seeks today to restore under its control. The other non-Russian nations are located in the Caucasus. The former western acquisitions during World War II and the Cold War also enjoy sovereign independence. This restoration of sovereignty came about largely because of the Western victory, so to speak, in the Cold War and the collapse of the imperial USSR. Now all these states possess incredibly valuable stores of vital minerals. The three Baltic nations still have enormous geostrategic significance where Russia is concerned, given their access to the Baltic Sea. Besides huge reserves of oil and natural gas, the other ex-Soviet republics are world-class sources of copper, titanium, aluminum, coal, phosphorus, and many other ferrous and nonferrous ores, some of which figure in defense production. It is no wonder that China, as a resource-hungry trader and importer of these raw materials, is now leaving a big footprint within these once Soviet territories. China, as a major buyer of such minerals from the ex-Soviet republics, seems also to be a future problem for Russia. This, given the PRC's enormous population, some ten times that of the RF, plus its current military buildup and the fact that by mid-century China is likely to economically and politically dominate all of Asia stimulates Russian intentions to close ranks with some of its former Soviet republics The western branch of these territories were part of Stalin's plan to retain the former tsarist and post-1939 Soviet imperial control over these territories. Putin's reference to the "catastrophe" of the demise of the USSR—and the loss of Stalin's Cold War victories—are of a piece.

The former imperial status of both tsarist and Soviet Russia raises an enormously important territorial issue that today affects Russian security. Moscow is facing the question of how to restore, at least to some extent, the sway and influence that Moscow once had over he important Asian territories. That Stalin relished governing an empire that included these Asian nations goes without saying. He sought imperial-type "security" at both ends of the expansive USSR, which was as wide as is today's RF. All his maneuverings with Nationalist China under the anti-Communist Chiang Kai-shek's rule during World War II followed by his support of Mao's Communist "people's republic" was always governed by how much influence Moscow could maintain over Beijing as the largest Asian power. By the time of Stalin's death in 1953 followed by the decade-long Sino-Soviet tension that included bloody border fighting, in the background was the issue of Kremlin control over the eastern portion of its empire. As to its loss of its satellites to the west post-Soviet Russia has been trying with only mixed success to keep NATO influence out of those east European and Baltic countries. But that is a long story.

The twin-headed tsarist eagle, adopted by post-Soviet Russia as its national emblem, signifies the way in which Russia still seeks to have influence in both directions, westward and toward the Far East. For Stalin, as for the post-Soviet leaders, influence translates into territorial issues. Under Stalin, Soviet imperial sway took the form of satellitization of the "borderlands" in violation of international law, countless treaties (see discussion below). These acquisitions, as noted by Russian historian quoted above, resulted from Western yielding to Stalin's questionable arguments and demands. One of the new post-Soviet *Russian* history texts speaks of Stalin's insatiable "imperial designs" after World War II. The Russian author, Yevgeny Anisimov, as do a few other Russian writers, adds that Stalin's "expansionist plans," as he calls them, helped bring about the Cold War.[3] This candid admission about Stalin's outright aggressiveness toward the two other members of the Big Three is hard to find among most of the Western Cold War authors.

In chapter 2, we assessed the factor of ideology. It figured strongly in the genesis of the post-World War II Cold War that was in turn linked to the Stalin Kremlin's expansionism to the west. It should be obvious to most readers that ideology was a determining factor in these policies as adopted by Stalin during and after World War II. His closest colleagues repeatedly asserted that in a new war, additional socialist Soviet-style states would appear on the map. As Stalin's chief ideologist, Andrei Zhdanov put it in 1939:[4]

> Around us lie small countries that dream of great adventures or allow adventurers to manipulate their territory. We are not afraid of these little countries. But if they do not mind their own business, we shall be compelled to use the Red Army on them.

> If you like a foreign province and you have enough force, take it immediately. As soon as you have done this, you will always find enough lawyers who will prove that you were entitled to the occupied territory." —Frederick II of Prussia

The recurring phenomenon in Russia history—namely alleged "protection of national security" from real or imagined enemies by means of arms which results in further expansion of Russia's borders—is shown in Table 4. After the Russian expansionism occur, the acquisitions become permanent annexations. Since 1939, for example, the USSR has annexed outright four of its former neighbors ringing the central Russian plain, has seized territories from seven more countries, and has made territorial demands on two others.[5] A total of 264,200 square miles of territory including (at the time of occupation) 24,396,000 people were acquired by the USSR during this period. Add to this list those countries that were brought under varying degrees of Soviet domination (excluding China),

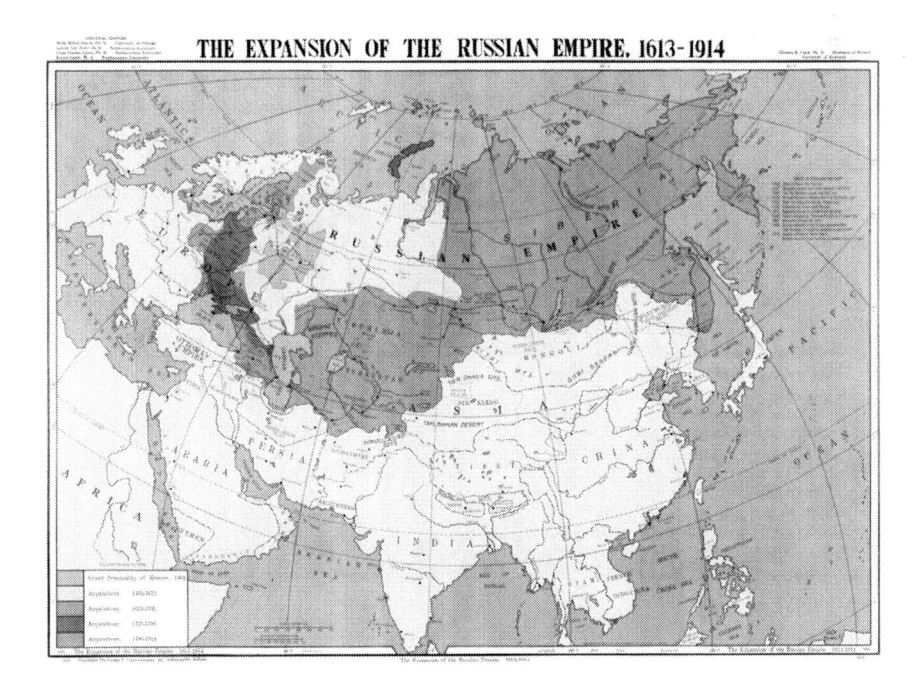

THE EXPANSION OF THE RUSSIAN EMPIRE, 1613-1914

Chapter 4

THE SOVIET UNION IN EASTERN EUROPE 1945 - 1948

Legend:
- Territory annexed by Russia 1939-1940, and re-incorporated in Russia in 1945
- Former German and Czechoslovak territory annexed by Russia in 1945
- States liberated by the Soviet army, and in which Communist regimes came to power between 1945 and 1948
- Russian occupation zones in Austria (evacuated 1950) and Germany
- British, French and American occupation zones
- The 'Iron Curtain' in 1948

The Russian liberation of Eastern Europe was quickly followed by the establishment of communist regimes, and an 'Iron Curtain' from the Baltic to the Adriatic. Communist rule brought national subservience to Russian policy, and the subordination of personal liberty. The cities of Berlin and Vienna were divided into Russian, British, French and American sectors.

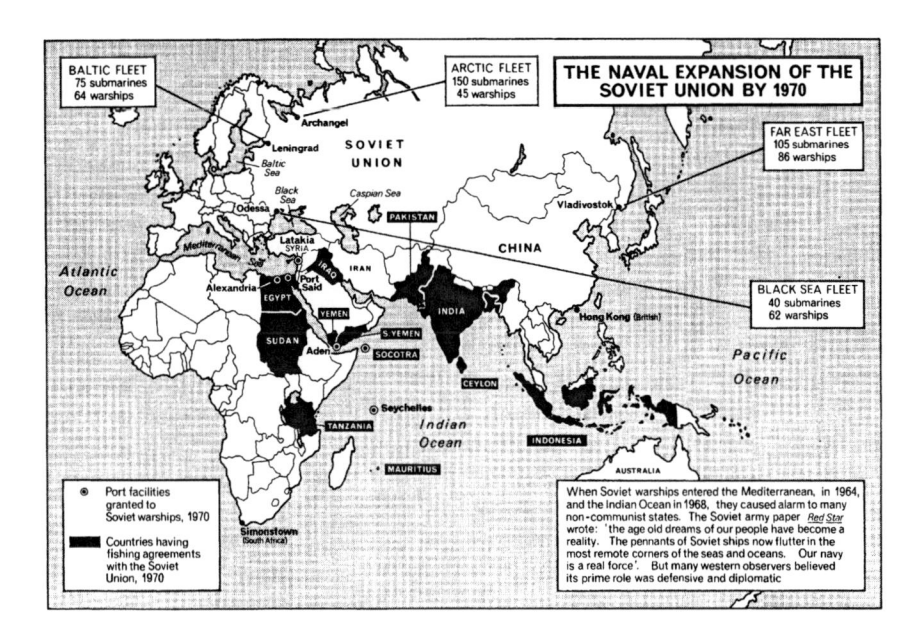

> **THE NAVAL EXPANSION OF THE SOVIET UNION BY 1970**
>
> BALTIC FLEET: 75 submarines, 64 warships
> ARCTIC FLEET: 150 submarines, 45 warships
> FAR EAST FLEET: 105 submarines, 86 warships
> BLACK SEA FLEET: 40 submarines, 62 warships
>
> • Port facilities granted to Soviet warships, 1970
> ■ Countries having fishing agreements with the Soviet Union, 1970
>
> When Soviet warships entered the Mediterranean, in 1964, and the Indian Ocean in 1968, they caused alarm to many non-communist states. The Soviet army paper *Red Star* wrote: 'the age old dreams of our people have become a reality. The pennants of Soviet ships now flutter in the most remote corners of the seas and oceans. Our navy is a real force'. But many western observers believed its prime role was defensive and diplomatic.

and the totals become 1,321,200 square miles and 123,657,000 people. Forcibly acquired territories were added to the Soviet empire by means of war or the threat of war. These blows of the hammer and sweeps of the sickle have given the insignia on the Soviet flag more than symbolic importance. To interpret all this as "defencism" is a grotesque misrepresentation of the facts.

As for the other bordering states, only Afghanistan—a mountain-locked Central Asian buffer state, whose main exports are horsehides and lambskins, and with a per capita annual income of about $50 (45r)—has not yet been forced to cede territory to Russia. Like Finland and Austria, Afghanistan has been sufficiently "neutralized" to satisfy the soviet-made laws of political physics for orbiting satellites and quasi-satellites.

SOVIET DOCTRINE OF EXPANSION

Going back to before 1939 and to the inception of the Soviet regime, Russian foreign policy under Lenin and the Bolsheviks from the very beginning displaying many of the attributes of its Tsarist forerunner—above all expansionism. Take the task of *reconstituting the old Russian empire* under the new Red flag of Soviet rule. Were the former forcibly ruled lands within the Tsarist empire to be set free from the empire after the revolution? Were the Transcaucasia, Turkestan, Outer Mongolia, the Ukraine, and so on, to be permitted to enjoy genuine national independence apart from the Great Russian center? If so, what of Lenin's prerevolutionary vision of the "worldwide union of the proletariat"? If not, what of the sincerity of the Bolshevik-supported concept of the right of nations to self-determination?

Despite his homage to state-less "proletarian internationalism," Lenin appears to have had some deep-seated, perhaps unconscious biases smacking of Great Russian chauvinism. Before 1917 Lenin's strong Russian bias was evident in his Russia-as-the-first-revolutionary-spark concept. Lenin also considered Russia's prerevolutionary "socialist intelligentsia" to be far more dedicated than their Central and West European counterparts, who tended, said Lenin, to act like "Judases" or be too corrupted by Western bourgeois society, which had existed for a far longer time in the West than in Russia. Likewise, after the Revolution, Lenin promoted the doctrine that the "Russian Revolution" (that is, the Bolshevik *coup d'état* of November 7.

Some undoubtedly would point to these apologias for Soviet expansion as examples of Russian messianism, perhaps even refurbished Pan-Slavism. However labeled, they frequently accompanied not only Red Army-supported restoration of the empire, but also post-1939 Soviet penetration of Eastern and Southeastern Europe, at one time an area of Tsarist probing as well. 1917) and the policies accompanying it should serve as the model for Communist parties in other capitalist countries, with minor adjustments being made for local particularities and contingencies. Moreover, Lenin seems to have conceived of a reconstituted Tsarist empire ruled by the Great Russians under the Red flag, including who knows what other additional nations, together forming what he called a gigantic "union of Soviet Socialist Republics of Europe and Asia."

Stalin was more specific about restoring the borders of the former Tsarist empire. Writing in 1920, he said:[6]

> Central Russia, that hearth of World Revolution, cannot hold out long without assistance from the border regions [formerly within the Tsarist empire], which abound in raw materials, fuel, and foodstuffs. The border regions of Russia in their turn are inevitably doomed to imperialist bondage unless they undergo the political, military, and organizational support of the more developed Central Russia.

"Clear, one would think," as Stalin used to say upon making an oracular pronouncement.

Lenin's rather more general pronouncement on the "further merging of nations" had implications for the small nations, formerly part of the Tsarist empire, which sought independence after the March Revolution in Russia in 1917 (Lenin's following remarks were made in 1917): "The proletarian party strives to create as large a state as possible, for this is to the advantage of the toilers. It leads to closer ties between nations and to the further merging of nations."[7]

Table 4.1.

Territories	Area (sq. km.)	Population
Rumanian provinces	50,200	3,700,000
Estonia	47,400	1,122,000
Latvia	65,800	1,951,000
Lithuania	55,700	2,957,000
Northern East Prussia	14,000	1,187,000
Eastern Czechoslovakia (Carpathian Ruthenia)	12,700	731,000
Eastern Poland	181,000	11,800,000
Finnish provinces	45,600	450,000
Tannu-Tuva	165,800	65,000
Former Japanese possessions (Southern Sakhalin and Kurile Islands)	46,100	433,000
Total	684,300	24,396,000

Territories under Soviet Domination or Influence

East Berlin and East Germany	111,121	18,807,000
Bulgaria	110,900	7,160,000
Czechoslovakia	127,700	12,463,000
Hungary	93,000	9,224,000
Poland	311,800	24,500,000
Rumania	237,200	16,007,000
Outer Mongolia	1,621,100	2,000,000
North Korea	125,600	9,100,000
Total	2,738,421	99,261,000

Note: Austria was under Soviet occupation until 1955; North Korea may be a joint sphere of influence shared by both Communist China and the U.S.S.R.; China is, of course, not dominated by the U.S.S.R. and is thus excluded; North Vietnam is both a Chinese and Soviet sphere of influence; Albania is not under the domination of the USSR and neither is Cuba. (All data are for status at time of establishing Soviet domination, not the population at present.)

The essential Marxist formulation that the proletariat's home is the entire world (Marx in *The Communist Manifesto:* "The worker has no country") was construed by Lenin and his associates to mean, in Russian terms, a "Soviet" of the proletarians of the whole world. Scholars debate as to whether Lenin himself condoned the more obvious neo-imperialist policies and actions of his own appointed Commissar of Nationalities, Stalin. However, the latter made no bones about the fact, either before or after 1917, that he supported a policy of coercion applied to the borderlands to rejoin them to the empire around the Great Russian center ruled by the Bolsheviks. It is hard to believe that Lenin could have been blind to Stalin's and others' maneuvers and endeavors toward restoring the empire after the Bolshevik *coup d'état*. In any case, the Vozhd, Lenin, did nothing to stop the step-by-step reacquisition of the Tsarist colonies, a process that was largely completed by the Red Army and the Cheka (security police) before Lenin died in 1924.

One of the characteristics of this early Tsarist-like policy of expansionism by the Bolsheviks, which eventually carried the Red flag and strong Soviet influence beyond the borders of the Tsarist empire (see Table 4), was the appeal addressed to Russian national security. This argument was offered by some of the top officials in Lenin's cabinet, the Council of People's Commissars.

We have already referred to Stalin's statement in 1920 that the center "cannot hold out long without assistance from the border regions." Similarly, several other top Bolsheviks after 1917 voiced concern about the "necessity" (in terms of Russian national security) of bringing the borderlands within the Great Russian orbit. Both this idea and an updated "dialectical" interpretation of the "white man's burden" are suggested by the following statement made by a member of Lenin's Politburo, Grigory Yevseyevich Zinoviev:[8] "We cannot do without the petroleum of Azerbaijan or the cotton of Turkestan. We take these products which are necessary for us, not as former exploiters, but as older brothers bearing the torch of civilization. Another characteristic explanation given by the Soviet leaders for this early period of Soviet expansion (1918–1922) was the conception of Russia as the savior and giver of progress to underdeveloped regions.

In the center or Europe, of course, there could be no reference to "borderlands," least of all reassertion of Tsarist legitimacy even as applied to Bulgaria, where the Tsars had been particularly active for centuries. When it came to the former Tsarist possession of the Kurile Islands, Stalin was not above reclaiming the islands on the basis of prior Tsarist suzerainty. As the Yalta agreement asserted, "The former rights of Russia violated by the treacherous attack of Japan in 1904 shall be restored."[9] Instead, the apologetic keynote became "liberation." The Soviet armies had "liberated" the peoples of Eastern and Southeastern Europe, say Soviet pamphlets and history books, bringing to them a higher civilization. The following quotations from Soviet sources convey these ideas:

- "The rise of the states of People's Democracy was assured by the averting by the Soviet Army of Anglo-American interference and civil war."[10]
- "The Soviet Army, which did not allow the bourgeoisie to seize power and which helped the toiling masses seize power in their hands."[11]
- "The armed might of the great Soviet Union . . . smashed the landlords' and capitalists anti-popular state power. . . . Relying on the Soviet Union, our people began building the foundations of Socialism."[12]
- Stalin had predicted exegetically in 1934 that the spread of world war throughout Europe would definitely change the postwar political complexion of the Continent in favor of Communist civilization. As he told the Seventeenth Party Congress in Moscow on January 26, 1934: "The war," Stalin said, "will certainly unleash revolution and put in question the very existence of capitalism in a number of countries, as was the case in the first imperialist war [World War I. . . . Let not the bourgeoisie blame us if on the morrow of the outbreak of such a war they miss certain ones of the governments that are near and dear to them, and who are today happily ruling by the grace of God. . . . There is no doubt that a second war against the USSR will lead . . . to a revolution in a number of countries of Europe and Asia and to the overthrow of the bourgeois-landowner governments in these countries."

We have reviewed Soviet doctrinal and propaganda treatment of both pre- and post-1939 Soviet expansion. Now we'll examine chronologically several case histories of this mode of Russian behavior toward foreign nations, more particularly toward *neighboring* countries. In some instances, the assumed or actual threats to Russia's national security—a rationalization often accompanying restoration of the empire—are offered as excuses by the soviets for the given expansion. Note also that in most cases the expansion has been a phase of a larger strategic plan, whether defensive or offensive in nature, as applied to an area of actual or impending military conflict.

The history of this Soviet expansion, the subject of the case histories which follow, is important for understanding, first, the diplomatic divergence that developed between the United States and the Soviet Union after World War II and, second, the brief period of "strange alliance" in that war. Even earlier, before Soviet involvement in the war, when the Stalin-directed Communist International (dissolved in 1943) ordered Communists in the United States to "sabotage" the American war industry, U.S. public opinion and the policy makers in Washington found plenty in the sSoviet record—dating all the way back to 1917—on which to base an anti-Soviet position.

Finland

"The secession of Poland and Finland [from the Russian Empire] after the victory of Socialism can only be of very short duration," wrote Lenin in 1916.[13] As it turned out, Lenin was partly right, if one counts the mere twenty-two years between 1917 and 1939, which was a period of nearly complete independence for Finland. He was partly wrong in that the Lenin government had made strong efforts to preclude secession and to incorporate both Finland and Poland into the Soviet Republic immediately after November 1917, but had failed. More prophetic in terms of future events—that is, the Bolsheviks' failure ever *fully* to restore Finland and Poland to the empire—were these words by Lenin before 1917.

> There are two nations in Russia which are most cultivated and, in virtueof a whole series of historical and social conditions, most differentiated, and which could most easily and 'naturally' exercise their right to separation [from the empire] . . . Finland and Poland."

After the Bolshevik *coup d'état* in November 1917, Russian troops were still in Finland. But so was a bourgeois government, which immediately reminded the new government in Moscow of its right to national independence on the basis of the Bolshevik Decree on Self-determination. Thereupon the Council of People's Commissars issued a special decree on December 31 recognizing Finland's independence. Commissar of Nationalities Stalin, however, appeared to be something less than satisfied with this course of events when he remarked to the All-Union Central Executive Committee.

> The fact is that the Council of People's Commissars against its will gave freedom, not to the people, but to the bourgeoisie of Finland, which by a strange confluence of circumstances has received its independence from the hands of Socialist Russia. The Finnish workers and Social Democrats found themselves in the position of having had to receive freedom not directly from the hands of Socialists but with the aid of the Finnish bourgeoisie.

Stalin added that this was a "tragedy of the Finnish proletariat."

Evidently encouraged by this and other statements by Soviet officials, the Finnish Social Democrats, at the time under the leadership of radicals, attempted to seize power by means of a Bolshevik-style coup in January 1918. They failed, but not before a civil war was unleashed throughout the little country. Soviet military forces, now loyal to the Bolshevik government in Moscow, were given orders to aid the "revolutionary forces" in Finland. As the *Small Soviet Encyclopedia* presents it.[14]

> On the night of January 28, 1918, a worker's revolution began in Finland and soon achieved victory in the southern part of the country which led to the formation of a Revolutionary Government on January 28. On March 1, the R.S.F.S.R. and the Finnish Socialist Worker's Re-

public signed a treaty of friendship. However, in May 1918 the revolution was crushed by the Finnish bourgeoisie with assistance from German troops. A reactionary regime was then installed. The Communist Party, which was established in August 1918, was forced to go underground.... The whole foreign policy of the Finnish government, up to the end of World War II, was oriented in a hostile way toward the Soviet government.

The Finnish civil war was fought with a ferocity that was to be repeated twenty-one years later on a bigger scale in the "Winter War" (1939–1940) between Finland and the USSR. Casualties in the combat of 1918 have been estimated at around 50,000. When the bourgeois government called in German troops, the radical Socialists and the Red Army forces were routed. Although some of its territory was taken away by the U.S.S.R. in the peace treaties concluding the Winter War and World War II (see next chapter), Finland has nevertheless managed to retain a large measure of national independence, enjoying the status of a quasi-satellite vis-á-vis its gigantic southern neighbor. Perhaps, as Lenin said, Finland could quite "naturally" exercise its right to independence.

Ukraine

The fate that was to befall the Ukraine, a "fraternal Slavic nation," was quite different from that of Finland, the non-Slavic neighbor to the north. As in Finland and the other borderlands, the overthrow of the Tsar in March 1917 and the establishment of the Provisional Government under Prince Georgi Yevgenyevich Lvov lit the fires of national independence in the Ukraine. In Kiev the Ukrainian Central Rada (Rada means council) was formed in March 1917 with the support of the Ukrainian National Congress. During the summer of 1917 and right up until the Bolshevik coup, the Ukrainians enjoyed a kind of spontaneous twilight independence as some of the Ukrainian Rada officials talked of some future loose federation or confederation with the Russians. Apparently "reading between the lines" of Bolshevik propaganda and statements by Soviet leaders after November 1917, the Ukrainians immediately became suspicious of the new government in Moscow and its promises of self-determination.[15] Therefore, on January 22, 1918, the Ukraine proclaimed its total independence from the empire, the Ukraine's right to self-determination having already been specifically recognized by the Soviet on December 17, 1917.

With the counterrevolutionary "White" forces closing ranks in the Don region of the Ukraine as the Russian Civil War got under way, Lenin presented the Ukrainian Central Rada with an ultimatum (drafted and signed by him) giving the Ukrainians forty-eight hours to assist the Red Army in its military actions against the "Whites" led by Generals A. M. Kaldin and L. G. Kornilov. If the ultimatum were rejected, the Russians said, war would be declared against Ukraine. Scarcely a week following Soviet recognition of Ukrainian independence, and upon rejection of the ultimatum by the Ukrainians, the soviet forces launched an invasion.

At the same time, however, the Soviets were conducting peace negotiations—on the basis of foreign Commissar Trotsky's "neither peace nor war" policy—with the Germans, who relished the opportunity of releasing forces from the Eastern Front for quick transfer to the West where the situation was worsening for the Central Powers. The Soviet-German talks were begun on December 22, 1917. They dragged on inconclusively until the Brest-Litovsk Treaty was signed on March 4, 1918. (The talks had however been preceded by a two-month armistice signed between the Soviet government and the Germans on December 15.)

As Red military forces began to sovietize the Ukraine in January 1918, the Brest-Litovsk negotiations were finally brought to a close. The two-month term of the armistice ran out on February 18, at the same time ending the Soviets' Satan's Holiday in the Ukraine. The Germans thereupon resumed their operations in the Ukrainian "breadbasket," and the Red Army began to retreat. By the time the Soviets had finally signed the humiliating Brest-Litovsk Treaty on March 4, the Soviet forces had been driven out of most of the Ukraine, including the capital of Kiev. This also brought to an end the *de facto* existence of the Ukrainian Soviet Republic, which had lasted for three weeks dating from only a few days after the Red Army's entrance into Kiev on February 8.

The German occupation of the Ukraine lasted until November 1918. But by that time, Polish and German onslaughts during the year had weakened the democratic Ukrainian forces. In the winter of 1919–1920, with the Ukraine cleared of Germans and the Red Army campaigns against Poland abandoned (see below, pp. 41–42), the Soviet government was able to dispatch forces throughout Ukraine that succeeded in routing the remaining anti-Bolshevik forces. The Ukrainian Soviet Republic, whose *de facto* demise in March had never been recognized by Moscow, was thereby extended to the "liberated" areas.

The Rada's protests against Red Army interference contained some pungent language (protests from the Rada dated even as far back as November 1917 when there were already some intrusions made into the Ukraine by the Red troops):[16]

> On paper the Soviet of People's Commissars seemingly recognized the right of a nation to self-determination and even to separation—but only in words. In fact, the Government of commissars is brutally attempting to interfere in the activities of the Ukrainian government. . . . What sort of self-determination is this? It is certain that the Commissars will permit self-determination only to their own party; all other groups and peoples they, like the Tsarist regime, desire to keep under their domination by force of arms.

The commissars, applying the arms of the Communist World Revolution, had thus forcibly incorporated into the new Russia their first major borderland nation.

Other Borderland Countries

A similar fate was to await one borderland country after the other in the years to come, their aspirations to national autonomy to the contrary. *Belorussia* became a Soviet Republic, by somewhat the same course of events as did the Ukraine, on January 1, 1919. *Georgia, Armenia,* and *Azerbaijan,* all of which had lashed out against Russian domination from 1917 to 1920, were subdued by the Red Army between 1920 and 1922.By February 1922, the "revolutionary army" had forcibly ejected democratic or anti-Bolshevik governments and set up puppet Soviet regimes in the *Crimea* (January 1918); *Bashkiria* (November 1919); *Turkestan* (February 1918); and, as already mentioned, in the three *Transcaucasian* nations (1920–1922). Engels had written in the 1850s: "Russian rule for all its nastiness, all its Slavic slovenliness, has a civilizing significance for the Black and Caspian Seas, for Central Asia, for the Bashkirs and the Tatars" (quoted in Carr, op. cit., vol. I, p. 315). Details of this process of invasion, occupation, and sovietization have been given previously in several objective studies and will not be recalled here.

The Special Cases of the Baltic States and Poland

Before turning to the successful empire-restoration campaigns of the Red Army in the Far East, we will discuss the frustrated attempts to secure Poland and the Baltic States for the Soviet empire. These Soviet attempts are of particular interest to Americans because emigrants from these countries to the United States are numerous. These early frustrations may well have had a delaying influence on Stalin in 1939–1940, when the Red Army entered the three Baltic States *to stay* while Poland was severed in half by the Nazi-Soviet agreements of August 1939, then occupied and declared "non-existent" by the Soviet Foreign Commissar. When World War II ended, Poland, although not officially incorporated into the Soviet Union, had become one of Russia's most obedient satellites.

Estonia and Latvia: In both Estonia and Latvia, at the moment of the Bolshevik *coup d'état* in November 1917, Soviet regimes were proclaimed with the help of Red troops. But as the German armies swept into the area that winter, these regimes were destroyed and the nationalized properties returned to private owners. When the German capitulation came in late 1918, "bourgeois" national governments were established at Riga (Latvia) and Tallinn (Estonia). But Red Army troops (composed of both native and Russian soldiers) crossed the frontiers of both these Baltic countries, and on November 29, 1918, the Estonian Soviet Republic was proclaimed at Narva while later, within three weeks, came a similar proclamation for Latvia.

A new phase began when the British navy steamed into the eastern Baltic, with the end of hostilities between the Allies and the Central Powers in the West. As the Allied intervention in Russia got under way, the British joined in the effort to de-sovietize the eastern Baltic and establish a base of operations for a "White" attack on Petrograd. The Estonian Soviet Republic collapsed in January 1919, while the Latvian Soviet Republic fell soon after. "Bourgeois" governments were thereupon reestablished.

When the Whites were cleared from the Baltic area by the counterattacking Red Army in 1919–1920, the Lenin government decided to follow the precedent it had established I the case of Finland. It permitted the Estonian and Latvian "bourgeois" regimes to exist, since, in any case, these governments had not assumed an unfriendly attitude toward the Soviets. Peace treaties were concluded between the RSFSR. and Estonia and Latvia on February 2 and August 11, 1920, respectively. As a result, these two countries were left alone by the Soviets until 1939.

Lithuania: The third Baltic country, Lithuania, presented a somewhat different case. There a "bourgeois" government was set up during the winter of 1917–1918. The proclamation of Lithuanian independence came, with German backing, on February 16, 1918. But once the Germans had left Lithuania in November 1918, a "Workers' and Peasants' Government" was proclaimed.

Poland: The next phase came as the Poles invaded Lithuania in the course of the Russo-Polish War of 1919–1920. Vilna was captured, and the Lithuanian Soviet was disbanded. However, when the Russians succeeded in driving the Poles back toward Warsaw in the spring and summer of 1920, the Red Army retook Vilna. But once again, as in the case of Finland, Estonia, and Latvia, the Lenin government refrained from outright sovietization of Lithuania. Instead, it concluded a treaty of friendship with the "bourgeois" government in Volna on July 12, 190. E. H. Carr comments as follows on Soviet tolerance of Lithuania's independence at this juncture:[17]

> Lithuania, though slightly larger and more populous than Latvia and Estonia, was an almost exclusively peasant country without a proletariat and with only a handful of intellectuals. Its claim to independence, whether under bourgeois or under Soviet auspices, rested on precarious foundations, drawing the major part of its support, moral and material, from a large Lithuanian population in the United States. The main interest of Lithuanian independence for Soviet Russia was negative. Were Lithuania not independent, it was likely to fall within the Polish orbit; on the other hand, an independent Lithuania could be a thorn in the side of Poland. Here, therefore, it was of Soviet interest to

give the widest possible scope to the principle of national self-determination.

As for Poland (the largest East European country), the collapse of the three empires of Germany, Russia and Austria-Hungary in World War I signified for it the rebirth of independence. Under Joseph Pilsudski, post-World War I Poland sought to weaken the Russian giant "through the creation of a series of independent states in the Western area of the former empire . . . isolating and weakening Russia to the point where she could no longer be a major menace to her neighbors." Pilsudski was, of course, mistaken in thinking that *either* White or Red Russians would tolerate emasculation of the Russian empire which would reduce the Russian state approximately to its size before Peter the Great.

When the anti-Bolshevik Russian Whites swept through western European Russia in 1919, the Poles kept neutral, watching the course of events while at the same time opposing either White or Soviet control of these areas. As the Red Army retook territory from the Whites in the winter of 1919-1920, the undeclared war between Poland and Soviet Russia grew hotter as hostilities broke out between the Poles and the Reds, and in April 1920 the Polish legions launched their campaign against Russia without a formal declaration of war.

However, by the end of July the Red Army was successful in driving the Poles back to the ethnic Polish frontier. An alternative then confronted Lenin and his associates in Moscow: to stop at this point or to go on and invade ethnic Poland. They chose the more radical "revolutionary" course. The Red Army was thereupon sent into Poland under the leadership of Generals M. N. Tukhachevsky and S. M. Budyenny (the latter commanding the cavalry) amid propaganda cries of "Liberate Warsaw!" But Polish morale was high. Under Pilsudski's direction, a brilliant defense of the Polish capital of Warsaw held firm after terrible battles were fought outside the city and on the Nieman River(total casualties on both sides in the Russo-Polish War have been put at about 600,000).

As the Red forces retreated back to home ground, and with the Soviet soldiers underfed, poorly equipped, and their supply lines overstretched, the Soviet government in a show of ostentatious audacity offered "peace conditions" to the Poles. They were indeed extreme: Polish armed forces were to be reduced to 50,000 men; any arms not required by this small force of some two divisions were to be handed over to the Russians, who in turn would create a "civil militia to be organized among the workers to maintain order and safeguard the security of the population." Poland's foreign relations with all countries except the Soviet Union and Soviet Ukraine were to be specifically limited; certain directives were to be applied to Polish internal life. Meanwhile, Lenin spoke openly of Poland's becoming "Soviet."

But the grim realities of Soviet military defeat in Poland finally caught up with the heady political leaders in Moscow. On March 18, 1921, the Soviet government was obliged to sign the Treaty of Riga. By the treaty, which was by no means favorable to the Russians, Poland was granted Galicia and the western part of Belorussia, territories containing mostly non-Poles. This treaty, a "minor Brest-Litovsk," did, however, give the Russians a *peredyshka*, or breathing spell." The temporary sacrifices of a bad peach," Lenin was to say later, "seemed to me cheaper than prolongation of the war."[18] *But the treaty was annulled on September 17, 1939.* Less than twenty years later, the Soviets acquired what they had lost by the Treaty of Riga. Stalin had gotten his revenge.

Expansion in the Far East

Prerevolutionary Russia sought expansion in the Far East, often at China's expense, for strategic as well as economic reasons. The following sample of this pre-1917 attitude provides a backdrop for the *Soviet* Russian expansionism in the Far East after 1917 (the quotation is from St. Petersburg's *Far Eastern Revue* of 1910)

> "Our border with China is irregular and hard to defend, nor does it correspond to geographic conditions. The natural borders of Russia are the deserts of Mongolia, the Gobi [which extends into Inner Mongolia] and Sinkiang. These dead seas of sand can be compared to oceans separating peoples and states. If we lose sight of this, the Chinese . . . will build roads through the deserts to the immediate neighborhood of the Russian border; they will become so strong that they will begin to push us Russians back toward . . . the Urals. There are many weak points on our side of the border. Lake Baikal, for instance. China could easily advance into Irkutsk Province and cut our communications with European Russian and the Amur region."

There is only one way of guaranteeing Russian security in Asia and it consists in rectifying the Russian-Chinese border. The natural border of Russia would be a straight line from the Sea of Japan to a point east of Lake Balkhash (in Kazakhstan).

Outer Mongolia: In the course of the reconsolidation of the empire to the west and south of the Bolshevik Great Russian center in Moscow, detachments of the Red Army were dispatched to the Far East to acquire territory there "for the Revolution." Outer Mongolia became a principal target for Soviet empire-building.

Outer Mongolia, with an area of 592,664 square miles, had been a Russian protectorate since 1916. In 1917–1918 all ties with Moscow were severed as the Soviet Civil War commenced and as news of the Lenin government's declaration on national self-determination in November 1917 spread eastward. But as the Red Army became strengthened under the aegis of Trotsky, and the Civil War turned in the Bolsheviks' favor, the government in Moscow was able to send forces out to Siberia, to Outer Mongolia, which had meanwhile reverted to Chinese control, and stationed them there from 1920 to 1924. During this time Outer Mongolia became transformed into a Soviet satellite bearing the name Mongolian People's Republic, amid strong protests from China. (Peking's response was: "The Soviet government has suddenly gone back on its word and secretly and without any right concluded a treaty with Mongolia. Such action on the part of the Soviet government is similar to the policy the former Imperial Russian government assumed towards China."[19]). Soviet "advisors" were installed in every government agency and the Mongolian army was placed under Russian Bolshevik command. At the same time, the Mongolian economy was brought into the general Soviet economic scheme. Finally, with the backing of the Red Army and the Cheka, the Russian-dominated Communist Party was established within the government of Outer Mongolia as "the sole ruling party in the country."

Outer Mongolia affords an early example of Red Army coercion coupled with Fifth Column cooperation by native or Moscow-trained imported Communists, a practice that was to be followed later in the Baltic States, and in Eastern and Southeastern Europe. Forcible collectivization of private farms and meadowlands, purges of "bourgeois" officials, and one-party dictatorship—all part of the Mongolian scene by the late 1920s and early 1930s—became a precedent for what the Soviet armies were to accomplish in the Eastern half of Europe during and after World War II. Even the designation, "People's Democracy," used for Outer Mongolia, was to be applied to the Central, Eastern, and Southeastern European satellites twenty-five years later.

Tuva, called Urankhai before 1921 and renamed Tannu-Tuva in 1921 (by which it was called until 1934), had at the time of Soviet incorporation a population equal to about one square mile of the City of New York— 65,000 in 1941 (today it is 150,000). Living on plains between Outer Mongolia and Russia, the Tuvinians are mostly nomads and hunters. However, Tuva is rich in minerals (including gold and uranium) and is therefore of economic "necessity" to the Russian center. Moreover, because it is located in the zone of Sino-Russian confrontation and is claimed by the Chinese as their territory, it is of considerable strategic importance to the USSR and to Soviet national security in the present post-1960 era of the Sino-Soviet cold war.

Under Tsar Nicholas II, Tuva became a Russian protectorate after 1912 and was controlled and exploited economically by the Tsarist government; it was incorporated into the empire in 1014. However, during the course of the Soviet Civil War, "White" Russian forces were driven out of the area by the Red Army (1920–1921). As in the case of the other regions brought into the soviet sphere by military means, slogans were directed to the Tuvinians which promised them that Russian imperial hegemony would be abolished "forever." But as early as December 1921 an "All-

People's Assembly" led by Communists declared Tuva a "People's State" and adopted a constitution. When a spontaneous anti-Bolshevik rebellion of Tuvinian natives broke out in the spring of 1924, it was forcefully quelled by the Red Army and by the local GPU (security police), which Moscow had established in Outer Mongolia under the leadership of the Communist Mongol Quisling. For twenty years a Soviet puppet state, Tuva was incorporated into the RSFSR as an Autonomous Region on October 11, 1944. Today it is grim to anticipate that the Putin regime in Moscow might be contemplating a similar ruse for eastern Ukraine.

American Reaction

The conquests of the old Tsarist borderlands by the Bolsheviks were, of course, in clear violation of the Lenin government's pledge of self-determination for all nations issued in November 1917. But even before the Red Army began to fulfill its "revolutionary mission" of restoring the empire, U.S. reaction to the Leninist dictatorship had been far from favorable. Not only did the U.S. press and public opinion begin to display a Red scare soon after November 1917, but the Wilson Administration began to map out a policy designed to keep Russia in the war (which ran counter to the Lenin-Trotsky line) and to keep Allied arms from falling into the hands of the Bolsheviks. The result of all this was not only intervention and aid to the "Whites" (1918–1920), but prolongation and deepening of a distinctly unfavorable American reaction in general to the dictatorship of the proletariat in Russia, and vice versa. Soviet-American divergence thus ensured.

The first major contribution to this early expression of Soviet-American hostility in the United States was the Sisson mission to Bolshevik Russia in 1918. Edgar Sisson, a member of the American Committee on Public Information, had journeyed to Petrograd and returned to the United States in the autumn of 1918 in possession of documents which, he claimed, proved conclusively what had before been rumored throughout the Western world: that Lenin's "October Revolution" had actually been a German-Bolshevik conspiracy against the Western Allies.[20] Although these particular documents were later proved false, the fact was that Lenin *had* received money and other assistance from the Germans in order to make his return to Russia in April 1917. The reaction in the American press to the various misdeeds and would-be misdeeds of the Bolsheviks was loud and acrimonious:[21]

> "Filthy pocket pickers and despicable degenerates of lucre."—*Baltimore American.*

> "Bolshevism means chaos, wholesale murder, the complete destruction of civilization."—*The New York Times.*

Some of the reaction rose to an hysterical pitch, the grand climax being the Red scare and the famous "raids" by the U.S. Attorney General A. Mitchell Palmer, and such press statements as these:

> "It is only a middling step from Petrograd to Seattle." — *The Chicago Tribune*.

> "The Russo-German movement . . . is now trying to dominate America." — *The Saturday Evening Post*.

The next milestone in this primordial U.S.-Soviet Cold War came in 1919. This was when the Third International (Comintern) was established, and also the Communist Party (USA). Needless to say, the party line at the Comintern's foundation congress was radical. Worldwide revolt was loudly proclaimed, and the anger and fear it evoked in many Western countries was particularly high-pitched when it spread to the United States. The news of Lenin's "Red Terror" (the Communists' term) campaign inside Russia (which need not take quotation marks, since the terror was very real indeed) also got a semi hysterical press in the West. The Assistant Secretary of State Bainbridge Colby wrote to Senator William Wadsworth in November 1919. that the declared purpose of the Bolsheviks in Russia to carry revolution throughout the world. They have availed themselves of every opportunity to bring about the forcible overthrow of our present form of government. When he returned to the U.S. from his post in Moscow, Ambassador David R. Francis declared that the 180 million Russian people should not be left helpless and hopeless under the tyrannical rule of what he called a ruthless, conscienceless, and bloodthirsty oligarchy, that is directed by a man with the brain of a sage and the heart of a monster. The president himself, who had advocated a policy of neutrality toward Russia immediately after the Bolshevik *coup d'état*, now vigorously opposed the Soviet regime calling it "a little group of men just as selfish, just as ruthless, just as pitiless, as the agents of the Tsar himself"[22] (thus anticipating for example, the Ukrainian reaction to the events of December 1917, or the Chinese reaction to the events of March 1918). Wilson went so far as to report that "they are about to brand the men under arms [in the Red Army], so that they will forever be marked as their servants and slaves," and one U.S. newspaper reported, also inaccurately, that Lenin was about to order the "nationalization of women")

When the Red Army began to cross over into ethnic Polish territory in 1920, in the Russo-Polish War of that year as referenced above, U.S. Ambassador to Russia Colby filed stern messages with the State Department back home. One of these was a letter in answer to a query presented to Ambassador Colby by the Italian Ambassador to Washington. After answering the Italian query to the effect that U.S. policy toward the Russo-Polish War would be one of neutrality (the United States would neither recognize nor aid the White General Wrangel), Colby seized the occasion to sum up basic American policy toward Soviet Russia. The basic principles contained therein were to govern U.S. policy toward the Soviets for over a decade. The main points were:

- Sympathy for the Russian and non-Russian peoples struggling to maintain their right of self-government and self-determination.
- The right of the Soviet government to preserve its territorial integrity in European Russia.
- Nonspecific affirmation by the American people and their faith in the Russian people's eventually finding a solution to the grave problems confronting them.
- Assertion of the notion that the existing regime did not represent a majority of the Russian people (if it was based on the outcome of the elections to the Constituent Assembly held in December 1917, the notion was true).
- Indictment of the Comintern for its subversive plans and practices.
- Indictment of the Soviet government for failing to live up to proclaimed promises, such as, for example, the Declaration of the Rights of the People of Russia (to self-determination): "They sign agreements with no intention of keeping them," added Colby.

The Soviet reaction to this published statement by the American Ambassador indicated that the Soviet-U.S. divergence was shared on the other side of the world: The Russian Soviet government is convinced that not only the working masses but also farsighted businessmen in the United States will repudiate the policy expressed in Mr. Colby's note [to the Italian ambassador] and is harmful to American interests.

Indeed, amid continued mutual animosity in the press and in public statements, U.S.-Soviet relations continued to remain poor until, and even after, the Roosevelt Administration in 1933 gave diplomatic recognition to the USSR although U.S. recognition of the Soviet Union gave legal foundation to the many business arrangements made between the two countries throughout the late 1920s and early 1930s, no profound closing of the breach in U.S.-Soviet relations followed FDR's 1933 decision. Nor did any major change in the popular American attitude toward Communist Russia take place in the United States, excluding, of course, the small radical segment of American intellectuals who sympathized with Soviet policy. (Irving Howe and Lewis Coser, *The American Communist Party—A Critical History* (New York: Praeger, 1962), mention Dreiser, Dos Passos, Caldwell, James Farrell, and Hemingway among those writers contributing articles to a pro-Soviet publication; but, with the exception of Dreiser, these men had no extended relations with the Communist Party and were not members of the CP (USA)." It would be erroneous to assume," wrote the authors, "that because a writer contributed to a Communist literary magazine he was necessarily a member of the CP" (p. 281).Neither did U.S.-Soviet diplomatic relations undergo any major improvement before or after 1939. In fact, with the coming of the Nazi-Soviet rapprochement, the joint German-Russian partition of Poland, and the Soviet attack on Finland (all of which occurred late in 1939 or six years following recognition), these relations took a distinctly downward turn from which they did not recover—and then only partially—until the opening of the "strange-alliance" era in American-Russian relations in 1941–1945.

Prewar, Wartime, Postwar Soviet Expansion

> "The victorious proletariat of one country, in the event of necessity, even [comes out] with force against the exploiting classes and their governments." —Josef Stalin

Soviet policy in the period immediately preceding the treacherous June 22, 1941, attack by the Germans against the other the cosigner of the Nazi-Soviet Nonaggression Pact (August 1939) sent U.S.-Soviet relations into a tailspin. Not only on the diplomatic level, but on the popular level as well, these relations underwent a freeze. The backlash even involved Communist Party members and sympathizers in the United States, who became disgusted and disillusioned, they said publicly, with the advent of a friendship pact concluded between the "democratic" Soviet power and the German Fascists.[23] Even more disturbing, at least to the U.S. Department of State, and ultimately to the public at large, were the expansionistic policies launched by Stalin immediately after the signing of the Nazi-Soviet Pact, and continued during World War II and into the postwar period.

Expansion Under the Nazi-Soviet Pact of August 1939

The government of the USSR in March 1939 took the initiative in reaching what seemed at the time to be a mutually profitable agreement with Nazi Germany. In his speech at the Eighteenth CPSU (b) Congress on March 10, 1939, Josef Stalin hinted at a rapprochement with Germany and evoked the following response from German Foreign Minister Joachim von Ribbentrop: "Marshal Stalin . . . expressed a desire to foster better relations with Germany."[24] Later, Stalin himself admitted that he had hoped for this response.[25]

Eastern Poland, Finland, the Baltic States, and the Balkans

Under the terms of the Nazi-Soviet Pact concluded at Moscow on August 23, 1939, Hitler guaranteed to Stalin eastern Poland along the rivers Narew, Vistula, and San, and consigned to the Soviet sphere of interest Finland, the three Baltic States—Estonia, Latvia, and Lithuania—and, tacitly, Bessarabia.

Eastern Poland

On September 17, 1939, Red Army troops invaded the area marked out in the Nazi-Soviet agreement for Soviet occupation of eastern Poland. Soviet Foreign Commissar Molotov attempted to justify the invasion in terms which, according to the 1933 Litvinov definition of aggression, were unwarranted. He said on September 17–18 that Red Army troops moved into Poland (1) to "extend a helping hand to our brother Ukrainians and brother White Russians who live in Poland"; (2) "to help the Polish population to reconstruct the conditions of its peaceful existence"; and finally, (3) on the grounds that "the Polish state and its government have, in fact, ceased to exist" and therefore all Polish-Soviet agreements including the nonaggression convention of July 1933, concluded between Poland and the USSR plus seven other states had likewise ceased to be in force.

All such pretexts had been ruled out by the disingenuous Litvinov definition of aggression in the League of Nations in 1933.

One should note that in Molotov's three-point explanation there is no reference to Russian national interest or national security. This obviously stemmed from the fact that no such admission probably could have been stressed in the atmosphere of the period 1939–1940, a period of supposedly ensuring German and Soviet amity, the Germans and Russians having just signed a friendship and nonaggression pact. The truth is, however, that national security as well as expansionism were uppermost among the motivations for the Soviet push into Poland, if not for the nonaggression pact itself. The second motivation, of course, was traditional Russian expansion, a characteristic Russian form of service to the *national interest*.

In the immediate postwar period, on the other hand, Soviet and Polish history books and commemorative articles noted the various Communist milestones in Poland. They referred to Soviet "national security" interests but failing to mention, Soviet ideologically inspired expansionism as the motivation for the Soviet invasion and occupation of eastern Poland in September 1939. For example, *Kommunist* (USSR), No. 1 (January 1969), asserted:

> Under conditions of the open preparations for war in Europe, it was crucial for the USSR to undertake whatever measures are necessary to postpone the danger of an immediate military conflict—a postponement which was to prove later to be of invaluable assistance in routing the Hitlerite hordes. Namely in this military and political situation, the Non-Aggression Pact was signed by the USSR and Germany. . . . Not a single Polish party-in-exile during the period of [Soviet and German]

occupation was able clearly to determine the road to Polish renascence... in fraternal, class solidarity with the USSR.

N.B., above: "Not a single Polish party-in-exile was able clearly to determine the road to Polish renascence." This is a typical piece of Stalin perfidy. The Western Allies simply let it pass as do some Cold War authors.

Neither Polish nor Soviet publications for over fifteen years have cited Molotov's imperial- and imperialistic-sounding statement in August 1939, that the "Polish state and its government have, in fact, ceased to exist." Rather, they stress the fact that history was eventually to bear out that it was crucial for the USSR to make the various Soviet decisions at the time to "stall Hitler" by means of verbal and written assurances and grants of territory (nearly half of Poland), and later with mutually agreed-to spheres of influence to be exploited by Germany and the USSR in perpetuity (discussed between the Germans and Russians in 1940).

After Khrushchev's ouster in October 1964, Soviet historiography, as directed by the party, began to revise its treatment of Josef Stalin. It began to refer to him as an outstanding war and postwar leader. Soviet ideology gradually dismantled Khrushchev's totally-negative, fabricated depiction of Stalin as a war leader. In the January, No 2 (1969) issue of *Kommunist* (USSR), one reads the following: "There is a not a grain of truth in the erroneous assertions about his [Stalin's] military incompetence, about his leadership during the war by means of a 'globe,' which have been seized upon and disseminated by foreign falsifiers of history." *Kommunist* does not mention that the source for imputing incompetence in military matters to Stalin belongs to Khrushchev, who denounced Stalin at the Twentieth Party Congress in 1956 and who mentioned the "globe."

Finland

After Poland, the next Soviet target for Russian expansion was Finland. Demands were made by the Soviet government in October 1939, for cession to the USSR of Finnish territory, partly on the grounds of the territory's importance to Russian national security. Negotiations ensued during the month, with the Finnish government agreeing too many concessions and compromises with the Soviet government. But when the Soviet government failed by diplomatic pressure alone to win as extensive an amount of Finnish territory as it demanded, it chose to resort to force "by which great historical questions are solved," to quote Lenin. A border incident was manufactured by the Soviets. And when the Finnish government proposed establishing a commission to investigate the incidents, the Soviet government refused. Instead, two days later (November 30, 1939) the Kremlin bombed Helsinki, and Red Army troops crossed the

Finnish border, thus violating international law and the Soviet-Finnish Non-Aggression Treaty of January 21, 1932.

In the course of the Red invasion of Finnish territory, the Soviets resorted forcibly to installing a puppet government in the village of Terijoki, near the Soviet-Finnish border. The regime, headed by Otto V. Kuusinen and called the Democratic Republic of Finland (or the "People's Government of Finland"), immediately concluded a pact of assistance and friendship with the USSR. on December 2, 1939. Foreign Commissar Molotov informed the League of Nations that any other government in Finland was unrepresentative of the Finnish people. And he refused, in the name of the Soviet government, to allow the League to study the continuing war situation there or to mediate it, thereby leading to the expulsion of the USSR. from the League of Nations. Instead, the Finnish Communist government in Red Army-conquered territory pledged itself to support any further "actions by the Red Army on the territory of Finland."

Thus, the war in Finland continued. But when the Red Army began piling up huge losses in men and material, and the USSR was *in danger of embroiling itself in a large-scale war with the protesting anti-Axis Western powers,* the Soviet government sought in January 1940 to end hostilities and negotiate an advantageous peace. After 105 days of the "Winter War," a peace was arranged on March 12, 1940, by which Finland lost all of the Karelian Isthmus, including Vyborg (Viipuri) and the northern and western shores of Lake Ladoga; made other territorial cessions to the USSR, including Kuolajarvi; ceded part of the Rybachi and Sredni Peninsulas and some islands in the Gulf of Finland; and leased the cape of Hanko and surrounding waters to the USSR for thirty years. In place of the People's Government of Finland, the Soviets substituted an enlarged Karelo-Finnish Soviet Socialist Republic.

By the armistice of September 19, 1944, and the peace treaty of February 10, 1947—in the latter of which the Western powers' foreign ministers had only a consultative voice—the USSR gained still more Finnish territory. The Soviets acquired a fifty-year lease of the Porkkala area and its peninsula (187 square miles) in the Gulf of Finland; the province of Petsamo became the "Petsamo Region" of the RSFSR—its nickel mines and the warm water ports of Lunahamari and Petsamo to be exploited in future by the Soviet state.

Soviet expansion at Finland's expense unleashed a groundswell of anti-Sovietism in the United States, much of it to the accompaniment of "Finlandia" composed by Sibelius. "Finlandia," however, was *not* the Finnish national anthem. The anthem is entitled "Maamme" ["Our Land"] and was composed by the German-born composer Fredrik Pacius. The small *official* U.S. loan to Finland of $20 million (approved by Congress) was scarcely a measure of the popular wrath of ordinary Americans (very few of whom, of course, are of Finnish extraction).

Grassroots America showed an amazing concern for a small distant country through its generous contributions to the nationwide Finnish Relief Fund and the Fighting Funds for Finland.

The U.S. government, if somewhat niggardly about extending a loan to Finland, was lavish when it came to words of condemnation of the Soviets. President Roosevelt himself stated:[26]

> The Soviet Union, as everybody who has the courage to face the facts knows, is run by a dictatorship as absolute as any dictatorship in the world. It has allied itself with another dictatorship, and it has invaded a neighbor so infinitesimally small that it could do no conceivable harm to the Soviet Union.

Soviet Foreign Commissar Molotov retaliated against the various official American statements, saying:[27]

> I will not dwell upon our relations with the United States if only for the reason that there is nothing good that can be said about them. We have learned that there are certain people in the United States who are not pleased with the success of Soviet foreign policy in the Baltic countries. But, we must confess, we are little concerned over this fact, inasmuch as we are coping with our tasks without the assistance of these displeased gentlemen.

Cries went up throughout America to withdraw the six-year-old recognition of the USSR. Writing in *Collier's* in April 1940, former President Herbert Hoover, for example, demanded the recall of the U.S. ambassador to Moscow and declared that American recognition of the Soviets had been "a gigantic political and moral mistake."

Only when Hitler launched his armies into Western Europe—perhaps motivated in part by the fact that he was temporarily relieved of any danger from Russia on his eastern flank—did speculation begin to appear in America that some way, somehow, Russia should be enticed away from Germany. Some even went so far as to predict that goodwill might one day return to U.S.-Soviet relations, because continuing the quarrel on ideological grounds was too much of a luxury in the face of Hitler's aggression along the fringes of the North Atlantic world.

Meanwhile, until June 1941 and the invasion of Russia itself by the Germans, U.S.-Soviet relations remained at extremely low ebb, although some partial moves toward a new U.S.-Soviet rapprochement (despite the Nazi-Soviet Pact) were dimly visible in the late winter of 1940–1941 and spring of 1941. Russia's ambassador to the United States Oumansky informed U.S. Secretary of State Summer Welles in the winter of 1940–1941 of the Soviet interest in increasing its purchases of military supplies from the United States. Although the United States was fearful that such supplies would eventually fall into the hands of the Germans, Welles finally agreed to meet some of the Soviet requests, but only with Soviet assurances that the supplies, either military or nonmilitary, would not be transferred to Germany. Soon, increasing quantities of American wheat, cotton, copper, and petroleum products were to make their way across the Pacific to Vladivostok (note that this bit of U.S.-Soviet rapprochement preceded the German attack on Russia in June 1941).

To continue the Finnish story

Early in the post-Stalin period, when a reappraisal of some of the worst features of Stalin's imperial policy was undertaken in the USSR, the Soviet government executed a minor retreat with respect to its Finnish acquisitions under the 1947 treaty. In 1956 the USSR evacuated the naval base at Porkkala. Even in 1945, however, the naval base had become obsolete, military technology having made new advances and Eastern Europe having become the new avenue for a Russian *Drang nach Westen*. Perhaps today, with renewed Soviet interest in the advantages of naval power on the part of the navalist party General-Secretary Brezhnev, the Soviets may regret having made the 1956 decision to relinquish Porkkala.

The Baltic States: Estonia, Latvia, and Lithuania. Formerly Tsarist colonies and newly become independent states after World War I, the three Baltic States were consigned to the Soviet sphere of influence by the Nazi-Soviet Pact of August 1939 and subsequent Nazi-Soviet secret agreements of September 1939. Within two months after the signing of the pact, Soviet pressure began to be applied to the Balts. Partial military occupation by over four Red Army divisions began in October, precisely at the time of the signing of "mutual assistance" treaties between the USSR and the Baltic States, a characteristic bit of Russian deception.

As early as 1936 the close associate of Stalin, Andrei A. Zhdanov, First Secretary of Leningrad Province and "architect of the Nazi-Soviet Pact," had issued a warning to Russia's smaller neighboring countries. The statement indicated that Russia would not stop short of using radical means—that is, its armed forces—to ensure its national security. It was, in fact, such a rare and frank admission of Soviet policy that it had to be retracted a few days later. What Zhdanov had said in the course of his speech to the U.S.S.R. Congress of Soviets, on November 29, 1936, was:[28]

> Round us are small countries which dream of great adventures or allow great adventurers to manipulate their territory. We are not afraid of these little countries, but if they do not mind their own business, we shall be compelled to use the Red Army on them.

The Baltic States *did* "mind their own business," rejecting, for example, a Finnish offer in October 1936 to form an alliance between Finland and the Baltic States which was to have an anti-Comintern orientation.

With the Germans looking on suspiciously, the Soviets began to hint openly in the spring of 1940—the Nazi-Soviet Pact to the contrary—that the USSR would come to the aid of the Baltic States "in case of attack," as the Soviet newspaper *Trud* ominously phrased it on April 15, 1940. This caused German officials to note on April 22, 1940, that the Soviet government intended to incorporate fully these border states into the Soviet Union. And, indeed, that was what was in the wind.

Lithuania was the first Baltic victim. An incident was manufactured, as it had been in Finland. The Soviets alleged that Red Army men were being kidnapped in Lithuania. Proposals by the Lithuanian government to undertake an impartial review of the situation failed. Instead, an ultimatum was issued by the Soviet government. In it, Moscow made the patently fabricated accusation that Lithuania was plotting with Estonia and Latvia to enter into an anti-Soviet military alliance. It demanded the arrest of certain Lithuanian government officials and the stationing of Soviet troops in all major centers of the country. Invasion and occupation by the Red Army thence took place on May 28, 1940. Similar ultimatums were dispatched to Estonia and Latvia.

In all three countries, Red Army occupation forces and new puppet governments were established after forceful dissolution of native parliaments under the direction of the Kremlin through such "plenipotentiary representatives" and nefarious characters as V. G. Dekanozov, A. A. Zhdanov, and A. Y. Vyshinsky, all of whom were put in charge of sovietizing the area.

That something besides national security alone had motivated Soviet military occupation of these states was made quite explicit by the Moscow First Secretary Alexander S. Shcherbakov in his welcoming address to the new delegates from the Baltic States, July 31, 1940:

> The capitalist world is shrinking constantly while the frontiers of Socialism are expanding under the sun of the Stalin Constitution.

Foreign Commissar Molotov added his voice to the triumphant boasts about Soviet security-*cum*-expansionism:

> "It should be noted that . . . this population previously formed part of the population of Soviet [sic] Russia, but had been forcibly torn from her by Western imperialist powers at a time when Soviet Russia was militarily weak [during the Soviet Civil War]. Now this population has been re-united with the Soviet Union. The fact that the frontier of the soviet Union will now be shifted to the Baltic coast is of first-rate importance for our country. At the same time we shall now have ice-free ports on the Baltic of which we stand so much in need."

The above statements amounted to Shcherbakov's and Molotov's updating of Stalin's assertion in 1934 (quoted above) that a new world war would see "a revolution in a number of countries . . . and the overthrow of the bourgeois-landowner governments in these countries."

The Balkans Bessarabia

In the Balkans, a traditional area for Tsarist penetration, the Soviets assigned themselves "interests" in Bessarabia under the Nazi-Soviet agreements. Bessarabia, today a part of Soviet Moldavia and a potential bone of contention between present-day Rumania and the USSR, is a fertile area of some 17,600 square miles that had been a part of the ancient Roman province of Dacia. It was settled by Slavs in the seventh century and from the ninth to the eleventh century was part of the ancient Russian state of Kiev, a historic precedent lost neither to the Tsars nor to the Commissars. Upon the withdrawal of the Mongols from the area in the fourteenth century, Bessarabia became a part of the new principality of Moldavia. Bessarabia was conquered by the Turks, with the assistance of the Crimean Tatars, in the sixteenth century and remained under Turkish domination until the Russo-Turkish War of 1806–1812. By the Treaty of Bucharest (1812) ending the war, Russia acquired Bessarabia. But the Crimean War (1856) resulted in Russia's ceding southern Bessarabia to Moldavia. The Tsars regained this territory at the congress of Berlin (1878), with a compensation paid to Rumania in the form of Northern Dobruja.

The year 1917, as it had meant to so many other former Tsarist lands, meant for the Bessarbians, too, assertion of their demand for independence. Under an anti-Soviet national council established in 1917, Bessarabia proclaimed itself an autonomous republic. In June 1918 it became an independent state, the Moldavian Republic; six months later it voted for union with Rumania which was recognized by the Treaty of Paris in 1920. On its part, the USSR never recognized the merger of Moldavia with Rumania. It implied instead that the old Tsarist claim to the area dating back to Alexander I and the 1812 Treaty of Bucharest was still valid. Once again the specter of Russian irredentism stalked another area bordering on the Russian empire.

Moldavia

In 1940, backed by the secret Nazi-Soviet agreements, the USSR restaked its claim to Moldavia—with the help of the Red Army. By the summer several divisions of Russian troops under Marshal Semyon Timoshenko were brought up to the Soviet-Rumanian border, supplying the ingredients of tension and pressure as a prelude to invasion. Thereupon the Soviet government issued an ultimatum over the signature of foreign Commissar Molotov stating that the USSR had "never acquiesced in the separation of the Bessarabian territory from the USSR. Thus implying Russian entitlement dating back to the time of the Tsars. When the Rumanian government proposed negotiating the question, a Soviet note sent on June 26, 1940, ignored the proposal and instead demanded that Rumanian troops vacate the area within four days beginning June 28. The Rumania Crown Council voted 27 to 11 to bow to Soviet demands without an armed conflict. (The Czechoslovak government was similarly to bow to Soviet demands in August 1968—without a fight.) Soviet troops moved into the area on June 28 with paratroops and airborne tanks, which were followed on the ground by larger tanks, artillery, and infantry. Slightly over a month later (August 2), Bessarabia was formally incorporated into the newly created Moldavian Soviet socialist Republic, one of the then sixteen (now fifteen) Soviet Republics. (It is undoubtedly not lost upon today's nationalistic Rumanian Communist regime headed by Nicolae Ceausecu that Soviet party General-Secretary Leonid Brezhnev spent an important part of his political career heading the Moldavian Soviet regime. Relations between Ceausescu and Brezhnev are known to be cold, and Rumania demands for a review of the USSR's 1940 territorial acquisitions at Rumania's expense have been hinted at in recent issues of Rumanian historical journals.

Northern Bukovina

Similarly, in August 1940 Northern Bukovina, an area of just over 2,000 square miles and rich in arable land and minerals, was incorporated into the USSR (specifically, into the Ukrainian SSR). Unlike the acquisition of Bessarabia, Soviet occupation of Northern Bukovina had *not* been referred to in the Nazi-Soviet agreements of the year before. It was only by intensive diplomatic pressure that the Soviet government was able to induce the Germans to acquiesce.

Sovietization of both these former Rumanian areas was soon begun. All land, the banks, and trading enterprises were nationalized and, as in the case of the Balts, mass deportations of Rumanians to the USSR were carried out.

As has already been mentioned, the Soviet occupation of the several countries of the Baltic and Southeastern Europe after 1939 was—and still is—described in Soviet histories as "liberation" of nations and "expansion of the frontiers of Socialism." In 1939–1940 and by the agreement alone with Hitler, Stalin had gained *over 172,000 square miles of territory and 20 million people of various nationalities.* Additionally, as revealed by Molotov's correspondence with the German Foreign Office in 1940, Stalin had sought partition of the British empire between the U.S.S.R. and Germany and control of other lands as well. Realization of these grandiose plans was, of course, arrested by Hitler's world-historical, so-called double-cross—the invasion of the USSR on June 22, 1941.

However, Soviet territorial ambitions did not disappear, of course, on June 22, 1941, least of all at the end of the war in September 1945. As Stalin had indicated in 1934, Russia expected that a new world war would serve as the midwife of Soviet expansion. Again, the means to be used for this expansion by the Russians were their armies. Again, too, the pattern of (1) *invasion and subjugation of parts of Russia by an enemy* followed by (2) *further expansion by the Russians* was revealed—in the case of (2)—from 1944 to 1948.

Soviet Expansion, 1940–1946

With the Soviet armies stationed in Bulgaria, Poland, Czechoslovakia, East Germany, Hungary, Rumania, Manchuria in North China, and North Korea (but notably not in Yugoslavia and Albania), leverage was thereby acquired by which the Soviet government could apply pressure to control these areas and convert them into virtual duchies of the Soviet empire. The use of force for Russian imperial purposes ran counter to a number of protocols of the Yalta agreements (Crimean Conference) as well as other verbal or written agreements with the Western Allies, and treaties with the countries directly involved in the expansion. Here again, Soviet expansionism caused alarm within U.S. government circles, which eventually spread to the population at large, thus widening the divergence between the two countries.

Satellite-Building in Eastern and Central Europe

Perhaps the first East European country to be subjected to Soviet interference on a large scale after World War II was Poland. Soviet activities there, in fact, provided the first instance of Soviet violation of the Yalta agreements and thereby evoked alarm and disillusionment in President Franklin D. Roosevelt. President Roosevelt said of this behavior, as quoted by James F. Byrnes in *Speaking Frankly* from a message from FDR to Generalissimo Stalin dated April 1, 1945, or just eleven days before the president's death:

> The concern with which I view the development of events ... the lack of progress made in the carrying out, which the world expects, of the political decisions which we reached at Yalta, particularly those relating to the Polish question ... any such solution which would result in a thinly disguised continuation of the present government [the Communist Lublin government] would be entirely unacceptable, and would cause our people to regain the Yalta agreement as a failure.

In the same message, President Roosevelt expressed disappointment in the failure of Soviet occupation authorities to carry out the Yalta provisions in Rumania as well.

A pattern of seizure became apparent for Bulgaria, Czechoslovakia, East Germany, Hungary, and Rumania:

- Red Army occupation in the course of the prosecution of the war against Nazi Germany

- Infiltration of policy and army by Communists, installed in their positions by Soviet occupation plenipotentiaries
- Seizure of power by the Communist Party followed by a short period of tenuous coalition government including Communists and non-Communists in the cabinet, but with the Communists holding key portfolios
- Overthrow of coalition, setting up of outright Communist regime; purgings of Social Democrats, moderate and "nationalist" Communists, and others opposed to strict adherence to Moscow's direction in all major policy decisions, foreign and domestic
- Sovietization of the country, the USSR serving as the model

This pattern was followed to the accompaniment of promises by Stalin personally that non-Communist parties, within and without the East European countries' governments, would be allowed to function. For example, in his answer to Winston Churchill's Fulton, Missouri, "iron curtain" speech of March 5, 1946, Stalin referred to alleged East European "coalitions" consisting of "from four to six parties." *"If the Opposition is more or less loyal,"* Stalin was quoted in *Pravda*, March 14, 1946, saying, *"it is given the right to participate in the government."*[29] Yet "loyal" in Stalin's lexicon meant pro-Communist, supporting without question the policies laid down by the Soviet-led Communist Information Bureau (Cominform) and the Moscow-based Information Department of the Party Central Committee.

All promises to the contrary, however, Lenin's basic attitude toward multiparty parliamentary government expresses the essential Soviet view for carrying out the aforementioned five-point pattern:[30]

Lenin: "No parliament can under any circumstances be for Communists an arena of struggle for reforms for betterment of the situation of the working class. . . . The only solution Communist-style is utilizing bourgeois state institutions for their destruction."

Rumania may be regarded as an example of this Leninist outlook and of carrying out phases one, two, and three of this pattern, in which the role of the Red Army was crucial, or "exporting socialism on the tips of bayonets." On April 2, 1944, Foreign Minister Molotov made a misleading statement on the current Soviet policy toward Rumania in which he disclaimed any Soviet intention of interfering in Rumania's political or social system after World War II. The 1944 Soviet promise to Rumania was made suspect by the fact that in the 1939 Nazi-Soviet promise to Rumania was made suspect by the fact that in the 1939 Nazi-Soviet agreement and in secret Nazi-Soviet correspondence (until June 1941), not only Northern Bukovina but *all* of Bukovina had been unsuccessfully demanded by the Kremlin to be included in the Soviet "sphere of interest" along with Bessarabia.

In August 1944, King Michael of Rumania accomplished the defection of his country from the Axis camp by arresting the Nazi-sympathizing Rumanian premier Ion Antonescu and sending in Rumanian troops against the Nazi forces. The king also proclaimed over Radio Bucharest that his country was no longer at war with the Allies. A government was then formed in which many political parties, including the Communists, participated. One of the first acts of the new government was to declare war on Nazi Germany.

But the anti-Fascist, representative government set up by the August 1944 coup was not permitted to last for long. By the Moscow Agreement of the Allied Foreign Ministers (Moscow, October 1943), the Soviet Union was allowed chairmanship of the Allied Control Commissions to be set up in the ex-Nazi satellite states of Eastern Europe and the Balkans after World War II. On those commissions, the Unitd States and Great Britain were to have "consultative" representatives. Frequent complaints voiced to the Soviet Chairmen of these Commissions by the United States and the U.K. that the ACCs in East Europe were not supplying the Western Allies with sufficient information nor were listening to their consultation were ignored by the Kremlin and its plenipotentiaries. On the other hand, in Italy, the Soviet representative to the Allied Advisory Council there was kept informed. Moreover, no interference in the democratic processes of Italy was carried out by the Anglo-American occupation. For example, the Political Section of the AC in Italy was abolished as early as January 1945 and in the following two years the remaining sections of this Commission fulfilled only advisory functions. Two years later, at the Big Three Crimean Conference, in February 1945, the joint Declaration on Liberated Europe was issued. It stressed the *joint* responsibility of the United States, Britain, and the USSR for establishing democratic and representative interim governments in all occupied territories prior to fully democratic elections that were to set up permanent governments. These governments, the conferees pledged, were to be "broadly representative" on the basis of "free elections responsible to the will of the people"— elections that were, moreover, to be carried out under Allied supervision.

However, even prior to the Yalta Declaration on Liberated Europe— that is, from August 1944 to February 1945—Red Army occupation authorities conducted or condoned attacks by local Rumania Communists against the coalition regime under the successive premierships of Sanatescu and Radescu. Mobs led by Moscow-oriented Communists attacked public offices and led threatening street demonstrations. The Soviet occupation's censorship over press, radio, telegraph, and publishing houses (provided by the Soviet-Rumanian armistice agreement of August 24, 1944) ensured Moscow's access to these media for propagating only its own points of view.

In February 1945 omens of a forceful Communist *coup d'état* appeared in Moscow's *Pravda*, on Radio Moscow, and in the international Communist publication, *New Times*. Mob action intensified. The practically disbanded Rumanian Home Army (what was left of the Rumanian Army was in Transylvania fighting the Nazis) could not oppose the mobs backed by Soviet arms. Town halls, police stations, courthouses, newspaper offices, and factory offices were seized by the Communists. The "storm-the-throne" mass demonstration of February 24, 1945, led by the Communists resulted in bloodshed in the streets of Bucharest. Finally, on February 27 Deputy Foreign Affairs Commissar Andrei Y. Vyshinsky was dispatched to Rumania to deliver an ultimatum to the Radescu government. This, of course, was done without any consultation with Russia's two allies, the United States and Great Britain.

The ultimatum demanded a Communist-type "united front" ("National Democrat Front") government to be led by the Communist Party — the premiership going to Communist Dr. Petru Groza, and the Ministries of Interior, Justice, Propaganda, Public Works, and Communications to other leading Communists. When the young king at first refused to comply with the Soviet demand, new waves of Communist mobsters were unleashed to the accompaniment of threats in the Rumanian Communist press. Red Army tanks rolled through the streets of the capital in front of the Royal Palace. Several key buildings in the capital were surrounded or seized in a manner reminiscent of the Bolshevik *coup d'état* in Petrograd, Russia, November 7, 1917. With tension at the point of explosion, Vyshinsky again saw the king. After a stormy monologue, Vyshinsky emerged victorious. Vyshinsky was awarded the Grand Cross of Carol for his "services" by the Groza regime. Molotov admitted that Vyshinsky "helped in the formation of the government" adding that the Soviet government had acted because "there was very serious danger of disorder and civil war." But in the Litvinov definition of aggression in the League of Nations in 1933 such a justification was declared to be an unwarranted pretest for interference and aggression. The Litvinov phrase read: "Justification for an attack may not be based . . . on the internal order of a given state, for example . . . on the political backwardness of a given country." The king thereupon dismissed the government on March 6; Premier Radescu fled the country. A Communist-led "National Democratic Front" government was installed with Red Army tanks standing by. Phase three of the pattern began.

This Communist-led "coalition government" agreed on January 8, 1946, to reintroduce democratic civil liberties, which the Communist regime and the Soviet occupation authorities had denied the Rumanians since 1944. But in spite of this and the Yalta pledges made to the Western Allies by the Groza and Soviet governments, no such liberties were introduced, nor were the elections held on November 19, 1946, either free or representative of the country's will. Within a year Rumania was declared a "People's Republic." All non-Communist parties, except those following the Communist line, were merged into the single Rumanian Workers'

Party. Anti-Communist leaders, such as the popular anti-Fascist National Peasant Party leader Juliu Maniu, and Constantine Bratianu, head of the Rumanian National Liberal Party, and many other anti-Communist political leaders fled, were arrested, tried, and imprisoned or executed. Phase three was thus brought to a close.

The coalition governments were temporary Communist parties predominated in the coalitions until the end of 1947 and early 1948 when the overt "Dictatorships of the People's Democracy" were proclaimed in the Soviet satellites of Eastern Europe and the Balkans. Then, phases four and five of the seizure pattern were put into effect.

The hypocrisy of the tenuous coalition governments of phase three of the Communist pattern of seizure was pointed out in the Fulton, Missouri, speech of Winston Churchill, March 5, 1946:

> From Stettin in the Baltic to Trieste in the Adriatic, an iron curtain has descended across the Continent. Behind that line lie all the capitals of the ancient states of Central and Eastern Europe. Warsaw, Berlin, Prague, Vienna, Budapest, Belgrade, Bucharest, and Sofia, all of these famous cities and the populations around them lie in the Soviet sphere and are all subject in one form or another, not only to Soviet influence, but to a very high and increasing measure of control from Moscow.... The Communist Parties, which were very small in these Eastern States of Europe, have been raised to preeminence and power far beyond their numbers and are seeking everywhere to obtain totalitarian control. Police governments are prevailing in nearly every case ... there is not true democracy.

Expansionism of 1939 to June 1941

In fact, this expansionism was the principal cause of the opening of the U.S.-Soviet Cold War. In their anti-Sovietism the American citizen and most of his political leaders and representatives seemed oblivious of the fact that eastern Europe was actually a remote part of the world, as far as the United States was concerned. It seemed to escape the popular American mind that these areas might, in an old-fashioned balance-of-power sense, belong to the Russian sphere of influence—as Churchill was to recognize freely in his wartime and postwar dealings with the Russians. What seemed to bother and irk many Americans was not only the fact that various homelands of a minority of its citizens were involved in the postwar Soviet expansion (particularly Poland), but also that an ally of America's should "behave," as it were, as slyly and as unfairly as Russia had behaved—for example, in its abandonment of the non-Communist underground in Warsaw in 1945 (the Soviets had refused permission for Allied airdrops to the anti-Nazi Polish guerrillas). This reprehensible bit of Stalin trickery, about which native Poles still grumble today, was preceded by that other atrocious Soviet action, the Katyn Forest massacre of 15,000 Polish officers at the hands of the Russians. Americans were also worried that Soviet expansion would continue and eventually include Iran, Turkey, Greece, and even Western Europe.

As noted earlier, Prof. George F. Kennan wrote of this period in terms that were at times critical of the wisdom of U.S. foreign policy and the way it coped with Soviet expansion:[31]

> Let us remember, in particular, that a considerable portion of American Lend-Lease aid particularly industrial equipment, reached Russia [after 1944, or after the abortive Warsaw uprising]. It was after this date that both Yalta and the Potsdam conferences took place. It was after this date that we decided to associate ourselves with the Soviet armistice commissions in the Balkans . . . and exerted ourselves mightily to bring Russia into the United Nations. Would it not have been better to have paused at that time, to have had, then and there, the frank and unsparing political clarification with Stalin which the situation demanded? If that clarification did not give us real assurance of basic alteration of Soviet behavior, then we should have abandoned once and for all the dangerous dream of collaboration with Stalin's Russia in the postwar era and have taken every conceivable measure to rescue what could still be rescued. This might not have been much. It would scarcely have been Poland. It might have been Prague; and it might have been Berlin — Berlin in the sense that would at least have spared us the embarrassment in which we find ourselves today.

Resistance to Further Expansion

The Cold War set in as Stalin consolidated his gains from the war period and appeared to have designs on other countries outside the immediate East and Central European "sphere of Soviet influence." If, indeed, he did have such designs, he was balked in a number of areas.

In Greece

The Truman Doctrine of 1947, giving military and other aid to Greece and Turkey, helped the legal government at Athens in defending itself against Communist-led guerrillas in northern Greece; rebel Greek Communist troops were trained and armed by the Soviet satellites Albania and Bulgaria. In the post-World War II period before 1947, British military forces in the eastern Mediterranean area also helped in preventing the Greek-Communist guerrillas from seizing power.

In Turkey

Hitler-Molotov conversations throughout 1940 contained the Soviet insistence that unless Turkey joined the proposed four-power pact (between Italy, Germany, Japan and the USSR), its territorial rights in the

Straits and Anatolia (Anadolu) would fall to the Soviet government. Hitler refused such extensive conditions for the Kremlin's membership in the Axis. With World War II drawing to a close, the Soviet government renewed its attempts at gaining territory at Turkey's expense, although Turkey had been one of the Allies in the war. On March 20, 1945, the Soviet government notified Turkey of its interests in the Kars-Ardahan area along the border of the Armenian Soviet Socialist Republic. Turkey remained adamant on preserving its territorial integrity and political independence. As in the case of Greece, the Truman Doctrine providing aid to Turkey buttressed the country in its successful effort to resist Soviet pressure, which continued to be applied throughout 1946 and 1947.

In Iran

Also among the Kremlin's stipulations as its price for joining the Axis Powers in the four-power pact was designation of the area "south of Baku and Batum in the general direction of the Persian Gulf . . . as the center of aspirations of the Soviet Union." During the period of the wartime occupation of Iran to protect its territorial integrity from the Axis, Soviet occupying troops exceeded in number those of the United States and Britain combined. Interference in the administration of Iran and in its economic and political life by the Soviet government was repeatedly protested against by the government of Iran. When the United States had withdrawn its occupation forces, the Soviets had refused to withdraw theirs; Britain had retained its forces there for fear the USSR would seize the oil fields. Iran appealed to the Security Council of the United Nations in January 1946. Subsequent to this, Britain agreed to withdraw its troops and did so by March 1, 1946. But the USSR continued to maintain military units inside Iran, and even sent in reinforcements. When Iran again brought up its complaint before the Council (March 19, 1946), the Soviet delegation opposed putting the case on the Council's agenda, but in this effort the Soviet motion failed to win the support of a Council majority. The case was therefore discussed and the issue was thereby brought to the attention of the world. In the course of the discussion, it was revealed that the Soviets had demanded of Iran hegemony over Iranian Azerbaijan Province and a joint stock company for producing oil. No substantive action could be taken by the Council because of the unanimity rule and the Soviet veto. Iran thus remained in danger. Iran thereupon took military measures to end interference in the province of Azerbaijan, sending armed troops there on December 10, 1946. Thus, Soviet penetration had been balked, largely because of the Iranian appeal to the world tribune, and especially because of the Iranian show of force.

In Other Areas

Obvious attempts by Soviet army occupation authorities in *Berlin* in 1948, 1961, and 1962 to put an end to Allied occupation in West Berlin met with failure. The famous "Berlin Airlift" of 1948 and the refusal of the governments of the United States, the U.K., and France to give in to Soviet pressure prevented a Communist seizure of the whole city. West Berlin German authorities also succeeded in frustrating German Communist attempts at seizing the city government. A strong Western occupation policy in *Austria* prevented a Communist coup there as well, although various attempts were apparently made to bring Austria into the Soviet sphere. When the North Korean "People's Republic" unleashed its invasion of the Republic of Korea in June 1950, this force was met with U.N. force, and the Soviet-armed northern invaders were repelled. Use of force in order to Sovietize French Indo-China was met with French counterforce against Communist guerrilla warfare similar to that employed earlier in Greece. Communist moves against British Malaya, Burma, Indonesia and other Southeast Asian areas had thus far been blocked.

All of these Soviet or Soviet-backed moves—in Greece, Turkey, Iran, Berlin, Korea, and so on—resulted in further aggravation of the Cold War divergence between the United States and the USSR. The "proxy war" in Vietnam has had the same result but with the addition of certain compensating factors which seem to portend not only an end to that costly "local war" but of eventual rapprochement between the two superpowers. For the United States, costly in the neighborhood of $30 billion per year with 39,000 American lives lost in combat. For the Soviets, no lives lost, but an estimated $1 billion to $3 million per annum in military and nonmilitary aid to North Vietnam and the Vietcong. The Soviet GNP is half that of America and was strained to provide Soviet citizens with an adequate standard of living.

The Soviet record of aggrandizement, security-*cum*-expansion, and unfulfilled pledges and broken treaties is surely not good. It is perhaps understandable that neither the U.S. government nor the American people have found any solid basis upon which to build lasting U.S.-Soviet cooperation beyond pro tem wartime collaboration, the World War II "strange alliance" lasting a mere four years. At times, however, the U.S. has appeared unduly alarmed at Soviet efforts to build an empire, or at least a bloc of friendly nations immediately adjacent to its borders. From a moral standpoint, Soviet methods were, of course, deplorable. But within a strictly balance-of-power frame of reference and taking into account Soviet hypersensitivity about its national security (which is not totally a pose), Soviet actions before, during, and after World War II are a logical expression of service to the national interest, although in often rather extreme form. We can perhaps agree with the following cool assessment:

Stalin has led what purported to be a world-wide revolution; but to those inured to modern Soviet pretensions his diplomacy seems curiously circumscribed. His arenas were Europe and the regions of the Far East adjacent to the Soviet frontiers and amenable to Soviet control.

CONCLUSIONS

What conclusions can be drawn from this survey of Russian expansionism since 1917 a canvas that does not include the pattern of steady tsarist overland expansionism since the fifteenth century? Does it show a pattern of mere, passive "defencism"? Russian expansion under Soviet rule surely warrants the interpretation made by a few of post-Soviet *Russian* historians that the Communist regime was bent upon deliberate, serialized expansionism. It did not hesitate to violate the sovereignties of the nations it made captive. Still, a number of Cold War authors, including, of course, a majority of Soviet and some post-Soviet writers in the RF, increasing in number under Putin, fudge over this Soviet record of expansionism. They buy the Stalin line about "defencist" security and the Stalin argument of an east European "springboard" that seeks to rationalize Stalin's deliberately militant Cold War policy.

One wonders, Why this obfuscation by certain writers? My assumption is, ruling out deep-seated ideological commitment in some of them, that it is simply garden-variety anti-U.S./ugly-American sentiment of the type that has cropped up in recent years together with the perception of an "imperial" America bent upon being the "world's hegemon." The contemporary attitude, in turn, prompts an artificial, anti-U.S. projection back to the post-World War II Cold War period. In this manner of *post hoc, ergo propter hoc*, some writers impute blame for the Cold War on the United States or at very least paint the United States as equally blameworthy as the alleged co-initiator of the conflict. The fallaciousness and unfairness of this historiographic mythology should be obvious.

In books and articles by Melvyn P. Leffler, one finds an implicit, at times explicit indictment of U.S. postwar policy as being excessively militaristic under the aegis of what he calls America's assertion of its "preponderance of power." America, he alleges, as do some other contemporary Cold War authors, was simply power-hungry at the end of World War II.

NOTES

1. Vladimir V. Putin, *Moscow News*, Oct. 4, 2010.
2. Yevgeniy Anisimov, *Istoriya Rossii ot Riurika do Putina, lyudi, sobytiya, daty* (*History of Russia from Riurik to Putin: People, Events, Dates*) (St. Petersburg: Piter Press, 2008), p. 471. Current textbook used in Russian schools.
3. Ibid.

4. Max Beloff, *The Foreign Policy of Soviet Russia, 1929–1942* (New York: Oxford University Press, 1953), p. 78.

5. Richard Pipes, op. cit., p. 128 (see note 3 of chapter 1). Lenin preferred, for tactical reasons, to delete "Russian" from the name of his worldwide republic.

6. Josef Stalin, *Marxism and the National Question* (New York: International Publishers, 1942), p. 76. From a 1920 article by Stalin entitled "Soviet Policy on the National Question" written in Stalin's third year as Soviet Commissar of Nationalities. For a comprehensive résumé of the evolution of Lenin's and Stalin's separate views on the subject of national self-determination, see Edward Hallett Carr, *The Bolshevik Revolution, 1917–1923*, (New York: Macmillan, 1951), vol. 1, pp. 410–428.

7. V. I Lenin, *Selected Works* (New York: International Publishers, 1934), vol. VI, p. 6.

8. Zinoviev in a speech before the Petrograd Soviet on September 17, 1920. Quoted in Merle Fainsod, *How Russia Is Ruled* (Cambridge, MA: Harvard University Press, 1963, pp. 361–362.

9. U.S. Department of State, *Foreign Relations of the United States: The Conferences at Malta and Yalta 1945* (Washington, DC: U.S. Government Printing Office), 1955, p. 984.

10. Hugh Seton-Watson, *The East European Revolution* (New York: Praeger, 1950), p. 167–168, quoting Hungarian Worker's Party Leader Matyas Rakosi.

11. N. P. Farberov, "Gosudarstvennoye pravo stran narodnoi demokratii" ("Public Law in the Countries of People's Democracy"), a pamphlet published by the USSR State Publisher, 1949, pp. 14–16.

12. From the Preamble of the first Constitution of communist Hungary.

13. Carr, op. cit., vol. I, p. 286 (see note 6 above).

14. *Malaya sovetskaya entsiklopediya (Small Soviet Encyclopedia)*, third ed. (Moscow: State Scientific Publishers, 1960), p. 1018.

15. These suspicions were extended to the Soviet decree on "The Rights of the Peoples of Russia to Self-determination," November 15, 1917. The key passages of this decree are reproduced in Mamatey, op. cit., pp. 116–117.

16. Clarence A. Manning, *Twentieth Century Ukraine* (New York: Bookman Associates, 1951), p. 46.

17. Carr, op. cit., vol. I, p. 314.

18. Anatole G. Mazour, *Russia Past and Present* (Princeton, NJ: Van Nostrand, 1951), p. 472.

19. From a note of the Chinese Foreign Office, May 1, 1922, quoted in Eliot R. Goodman, *The Soviet Design for a World State* (New York: Columbia University Press, 1957), p. 60

20. Foster Rhea Dulles, *The Road to Teheran: The Story of Russia and America, 1781–1943* (Princeton, NJ: Princeton University Press, 1944), pp. 153–154. For a description of Lenin's involvement with the Kaiser's government in Berlin, see Alexander Kerensky, *Russia and History's Turning Point* (New York: Duell, Sloan and Pearce, 1965), Chapter 18, "The Path of Treason," pp. 301–323; or a briefer, more popularized account found in Robert K. Massie, *Nicholas and Alexandra* (New York: Atheneum, 1967), p. 442; or the longer exposition to be found in Adam B. Ulam, *The Bolsheviks: The Intellectual and Political History of the Triumph of Communism in Russia* (New York: Macmillan, 1965), pp. 325–329.

21. Peter G. Filene, *Americans and the Soviet Experiment, 1917–1933* (Cambridge, MA.: Harvard University Press, 1967), p. 59, for newspaper quotes. This book reproduces several interesting cartoons from U.S. newspapers. For my review of this book: *The Annals of the American Academy of Political and Social Science*, vol. 373, September 1967, pp. 244–245.

22. Dulles, op. cit., pp. 155-156. For this and following quotes in this paragraph.

23. *Trial of the Major German War Criminals: Proceedings of the International Military Tribunal* (Official Transcript), (London: H. M. Stationery Office, 1946–1948), vol. X, p. 267.

24. A. Rossi, *The Russo-German Alliance, August 1939—June 1941* (Boston: Beacon Press, 1951), p. 9. Of Soviet breaking of treaties and nonaggression agreements made with countries that were later occupied by the USSR. (e.g., Finland and the Baltic countries, Estonia, Latvia, and Lithuania), A. Glenn Mower, Jr., has written: "Treaties are instruments of foreign policy, agreements that embody arrangements that are to the mutual national interest of the parties to them at the time they are contrived. While an old principle of international law, *pacta sunt servanda*, expresses the idea that treaties are to be observed, another venerable principle, *rebus sic stantibus*, suggests that circumstances may so change as to render a treaty inoperative. In an essentially anarchic world, there is no one authority to pass with finality on the question of when circumstances have so altered as to release a treaty signatory from its obligation; and here, as throughout international law, each sovereign state reserves to itself the right to decide" [italics mine]. From A. Glenn Mower, Jr., "The International Morality of the Soviet Union," in Pentony (ed.), op. cit., p. 184. Mower follows a generally plague-on-both-houses approach to violations of international law by both of the large nation-states, the United States and the Soviet Union. He sees no difference, either in degree or kind, between the many violations of international law by the USSR. and the obviously much less reprehensible transgressions by the United States which Mower singles out—for example, by its proclamation of neutrality in 1793, the United States violated its treaty with France in 1778 which required us to assist France in its struggle with England—and one or two other examples of similar antiquity or irrelevance.

25. Ibid.
26. Dulles, op. cit., pp. 221–222.
27. Ibid., pp. 334–335.
28. Beloff, op. cit., vol. 23, p. 78.
29. Weeks, *The Other Side of Coexistence*, p. 58.
30. Lenin, *Selected Works*, Vol. XXV. Hitler said on July 18, 1930: "We National Socialists know that no election can conclusively decide the fate of a nation.")
31. George F. Kennan, *Russia and the West Under Lenin and Stalin* (Boston: Little Brown, 1960), p. 366.

FIVE
Cold War Clash Over a Postwar World

One of the underlying sticking points in the genesis of the Cold War were the conflicting projections of the postwar world made by the two Allied powers—the United States and Great Britain—*versus* that of the USSR. These differences hovered over East-West relations during World War II and came into sharp focus after the war. They became factors in the ongoing Cold War.

The verbiage—in the official Allied documents—concerning the nature of the postwar world was clear enough. Texts, on paper as they appeared in public indicated that the Big Three were in agreement, if hazily so that:

- Aggression against other states would be condemned, that joint action against such violation of International Law and the various treaties and documents concerning the postwar future would be enforced by the victors in the war through the United Nations.
- Jointly signed documents by the Big Three, like the Atlantic Charter and the Declaration on the Liberation of Europe, meant that the Allies, East and West, agreed that democracy, national sovereignty, and civil rights would not be violated as they so often were prewar.
- It was more than simply implied by the verbiage in the documents supported by the Big Three that democratic polities would replace all tyrannical, despotic ones, which were deemed to be the main cause of aggression in Word War II.

It might well be asked how President Roosevelt and Prime Minister Churchill could have possibly believed that Josef Stalin, the chief interpreter of Soviet ideology could have been serious in signing such documents. There is little doubt that on his part, the British leader chested his cards, surreptitiously, on seriously accepting such Soviet largesse lest he upset the apparently cooperative spirit that reigned at the summits at Teheran and Yalta. On his part, however, FDR entertained extremely optimistic and lofty if not fantastic notions regarding the Soviet Union and Stalin's postwar plans for his country and for the world (see discussion of the OWI guide book in Appendix I). As his top aide, Harry Hopkins once put it with naive optimism: "In our hearts we really believed a new day had dawned. We were all convinced we had won this first great victory for peace. . . . The Russians had proved they could be reasonable and farsighted and neither the President nor any of us had the slightest doubt that we could live with them and get on peaceably with them far into the future."[1]

Churchill added his own note of hopeful optimism: "Marshal Stalin and the Soviet leaders wish to live in honorable friendship and equality with the Western democracies."[2]

THE ROOSEVELT FACTOR

Roosevelt's behavior toward Stalin, with whom in correspondence he called "Uncle Joe," was marked by the following:

- The prediction that the Soviet Union was on an historic course of democratization as suggested, Roosevelt said, by various articles in the 1936 Soviet Constitution, known as the "Stalin Constitution." For instance, Roosevelt pointed to Art. 124 of this document and its promise of religious freedom as a positive "democratic" feature of the charter. The president did not reference Art. 126 in which the Communist Party is designated as the single "leading" core of all organizations in the USSR, political and social, thus making the Soviet Union a "party-state" or "one-party dictatorship."[3]

Roosevelt regarded Stalin's socialism as an "Asiatic form" of the New Deal. On another occasion, Roosevelt opined that he did not regard Stalin as an ideologue at all but as a "realist." As he put it, "Their word is their bond" (quote reproduced in Nisbet, *op. cit.*, p. 77). It is no wonder that Soviet specialists and former Ambassadors to Moscow, like Kennan and Bullitt, were so astounded by FDR's naïveté toward Stalin's Russia. Today over sixty-five years after the start of the Cold War, it is shocking to find a similar naïveté in so many of the recent books on the Cold War. Roosevelt was convinced that Stalin could see eye-to-eye with the Western democracies, that the USSR would inevitably evolve in a democratic direction. For his part, Churchill tended at times to be doubtful. Yet even he thought Stalin could be brought around. As late as 1952, deep in the midst of the Cold War and the war in Korea (1950–1953), Churchill proposed that the Big Three once more convene in a summit as allies as they had after the war. Not surprisingly, nothing came of this untimely notion.

STALIN'S "WORLD" VS. WESTERN PROJECTION

To the degree that Stalin believed deeply in the postulates and axioms of Marxism-Leninism—as all his writings throughout his life attest he did—there was simply no chance that Soviet Union under Stalin's and his cohorts' dictatorship would ever "converge" or see eye-to-eye with the West. "East is East and West is West, never the twain shall meet."

In international relations, a fundamental principal for a degree of amity between nation-states is their deep-rooted, collective agreement on matters of law, in this case International Law. Yet any scholar who is at all familiar with Marxism-Leninism-Stalinism's teaching on Law understands that an insurmountable gulf separates the Soviet concept of Law from that of the Western legal tradition.

This difference begins with the very basis of law. As Andrei Vyshinsky observes in his widely read classic text of 1938 (which became available to English readers only by 1948 under the title, *The Law of the Soviet State*) on the Soviet view toward Law and with reference to International Law, Western "bourgeois class law" is totally rejected by the Soviet concept of Law. According to Soviet theory, bourgeois law, as found in such concepts as that of International Law and the Charter of the United Nations, aims at one goal, defense of class interests as against those of the workers.[4]

Soviet theory of law and government also includes the idea of states' being an expression of bourgeois law as projected on the world community. Thus, their policies as bourgeois states will be "inevitably" aimed at defending class interests on an international basis. This bias prompted Jonathan Haslam, author of an admirable study of the Cold War, to observe: "The Soviets asserted the class basis of Soviet foreign policy. [There will be] no denial [a Soviet document stated] of Marxism-Leninism in the international sphere. [This] affirmed the abyss in East-West relations . . . and predated the summit between allied leaders at Yalta from 4 to 11 February [1945]. Churchill was all set for the worst." Cf. Jonathan Haslam, *Russia's Cold War: From the October Revolution to the Fall of the Wall,* Yale University Press, New Haven, 2011, p. 31. John L. Gaddis makes a similar point in his superb study of the Cold War (Gaddis, op. cit.), pp. 13–15ff.

These ideas may sound preposterous to today's readers. That is, until they realize that before the Progressive Era in the United States, especially at the local level, laws and law enforcement were, indeed, often aimed at protecting the interests of Big Business. Back in those pre-Progressive Era days, the courts supported the police in doing pretty much as they wished in breaking up protesting workers. So, this is not exclusively a Marxist idea. The phenomenon is well known to American historians and non-socialist critics of American Law. Of course, it is thoroughly un-Marxist and un-Leninist to cite the many root changes that have occurred in the concept and application of Law made in the West since World War I, from decisions by the U.S. Supreme Court down to the local courts. The Communists vehemently deny that under capitalism there can be anything like judicial fairness and objectivity. Yet in the twentieth century, law was deeply democratized and freed of economic bias in the United States and generally throughout the West. It was likewise cleansed, of course, of other biases whether racial or sexual.

In terms of International Law and institutions like the League of Nations or the United Nations—which is related to the problem of instigating cold wars—Soviet legal scholars rigorously refused to acknowledge the objectivity of these bodies. Least of all did they acknowledge that such a world institution should be possessed with the powers of compulsive jurisdiction and compulsive adjudication the way national and local juridical theory and practice do in civilized countries. In this as respects the League and the U.N., they were on target. Neither world organization was given these powers

Above all, the "first socialist state," the USSR, would never become a party to such a "bourgeois" charade as the idea of "world government" or a truly effective world organization if a consensus within it ever clashed in a significant way with the prerogatives of Soviet ideology and its foreign policy goals that Moscow viewed as enhancing the power of the Communist bloc that it controlled.

It might be asked, then, given such a divisive East versus West philosophy of Law, how could the USSR have possibly joined the League of Nations (as it did in 1934) or after World War II, the United Nations Organization (in 1945), with this hostile Soviet attitude toward Western and International Law?

The answer to this question lies in understanding the Soviet regime's "two-track" policy: That is, one policy meant for public consumption and conventional interstate relations *versus* the other principled track that followed underlying Soviet socialist "internationalist" goals that repudiated all "bourgeois" legal and political institutions whether domestic or international. Pacifist movements too, were among those so repudiated.

Meantime, consider how membership, no matter how pro forma in either world organization, allowed assertion of Soviet influence, known today as "soft power." Would not the Soviet presence in such much-publicized "world forums" as the League and U.N. help advertise and cater to the interests of the Soviet Union as well as promoting its socialist ideals? This type of political motivation was particularly obvious after 1960. This was when former colonial states in Africa and Asia acquired national independence and became a virtual bloc. As a result of this development, Soviet positions in the Assembly and Security Council resonated with active support for "anti-colonial" violence of the type sponsored by Communist-led, armed "national liberation" movements throughout Africa and Asia.[5] This group of "developing nations"" (formerly called "underdeveloped" nations) had become by the 1960s a formidable political force under the mantra of the "Third World." They actually dominated membership in the U.N. General Assembly. The term for such nations was first employed in the U.N. by none other than Deng Xiaoping in his opening address in the U.N. in 1974.

Obviously, both institutions could be regarded, as they actually were, just such useful platforms for promoting Soviet political ideas in terms of global politics. Besides, the USSR would always retain the power of using the veto over any effective measures endorsed by the League or UN Moscow but which did not support. Indeed, it held the record in the casting of vetoes in the Security Council.[6] This did not bode well for those who trusted that the USSR's presence in the world body would translate into global harmony.

Soviet policy positions in the League as in the UN often severely clashed in matters of principle with those of the "Western bloc," in particular with those of the United States. Even in the post-Soviet period, Russian policy positions in the U.N. often conflict with those of Western members of the world organization. Russian vetoes run parallel with those of Communist China. With the latter, today's Kremlin leadership declares that it has a "friendly . . . strategic partnership" that includes the partners' agreement on such matters as blocking "U.S. hegemonism" worldwide. It may be significant, however, that the term "alliance" is never used to describe this Sino-Russian relationship just as it was likewise omitted in the prewar Nazi-Soviet partnership, or "honeymoon," between August 1939 and late June 1941.

Finally, the Soviet projection of the new world after the war radically contrasted with the Western in other respects.. The former's projection was best seen in the political and social structures developed in the USSR as well as in the seized sovietized lands that the Red Army had occupied in Europe and Asia including the territory that is now part of North Korea. The following were the principal clashing points:

- The Soviets believed that one-party dictatorship and the Communist program for ensuring the "dialectical" transition from capitalism to first-phase socialism, then to the final phase of full-fledged communism (lower-case c) was the *model for all global societies*. Soviet efforts to help this global process along are well known. They took the form of the Comintern, then the Cominfom, and finally the Information Department of the party Central Committee in Moscow. In the period from the reigns of Khrushchev (1957–1964) and Brezhnev (1964–1982), Moscow was constantly increasing its material support for armed, Communist-led guerrilla forces worldwide under the mantra of "national-liberation struggle." Part of the bankruptcy suffered by Soviet Russia by the late 1980s was not only due to its huge expenditures on its own arms and overseas bases, but on its many-sided support of these ubiquitous armed movements throughout the Third World. All such movements included a program whose design essentially copied the Soviet Bloc system of totalitarianism.

- The "iron curtain" phenomenon, accompanied by the Berlin Wall, Soviet censorship (copied in Maoist China) and its anti-Westernism, and "spy mania," was overtly hostile to Western values of free speech and unfettered intercourse between nations. The totalitarian notion (exemplified, by the way, in the writings of Deng Xiaoping) of keeping the Communist-led society free of corrupting foreign "infection" naturally jibes with the idea of protecting one-party rule from any challenging political philosophy such as positively recognized in Japan or the Republic of China (Taiwan). Western ideas are obviously appealing to citizens under such regimes, as witnessed by the phenomena of their citizens' desire to emigrate, even at the risk of their lives. Most citizens, of course, are trapped. They lack the means to escape their virtual captivity. Others, of course, support the regime. Yet the whole Communist project of keeping their monolithic controls intact and free of what Deng called foreign "flies" and other such infestation from the West is aimed at keeping the society as safe as possible from foreign influence. The reaction to such authoritarian and totalitarian measures against free exchange and intercourse between nations is naturally resentful. It reminds many people of the idea of "Communazism," or the resemblance between the hated fifteen- to twenty-year period of the reign of Italian Fascism and German Nazism in Europe and that imposed by Lenin and Stalin and his followers over Russia and territories the Bolsheviks seized. This hostility, in turn, helped keep the Cold War in a frozen state. Even since China's "opening up" after 1978, numerous Soviet-style restrictions on Chinese citizens' freedoms exist in the PRC. These, in turn, prompt Cold War-type accusations against Communist China from freer societies. Which ire also impedes international cooperation. Today's Russia, too, displays holdovers from the Soviet past in terms of various restrictions against a Free Marketplace of Ideas.
- Also fueling the Cold War or any cold war between a nation with a liberal-democratic system vs. an authoritarian or totalitarian polity is the militarism generated by one-party regimes. This policy is sometimes combined with revanchist nationalism, which in turn helps bolster popular support for the regime. In the Soviet case, this took the form of Stalin's and his successors' virtually racist idea of

"Great Russian superiority."[7] This nationalist emphasis is again cropping up in today's Russian under Putin's heavy-handed leadership.

Authoritarian-type regimes enjoy a political free hand when shaping and executing foreign policy. Lacking the democratic principle of separation of powers and the democratically elected legislature's checks on executive power, one-party elite alone enjoys the exclusive power to make foreign policy and the major decisions concerning peace and war—these, without interference from any Congressional, parliament, assembly, etc. In his writings, Deng notes, as Soviet writers always did when addressing the question of Soviet centralism, China's absence of "interfering" separate powers, how such centralized authority that Beijing's rulers enjoy provides a Communist-type party-state with expeditiousness and dispatch that, as Communist literature likewise explicitly states, are lacking in the slow-moving, excessively discursive liberal democratic polities—to their disadvantage.

CLASHES BETWEEN "CIVILIZATIONS"

Finally, a widely held view well-known scholars in the field of the history of civilizations goes that between a number of such civilizations today there are significant, to use Samuel Huntington's term, "fault lines."

Samuel P. Huntington resurrected an old controversy in the study of international affairs: the relationship between "microcosmic" and "macrocosmic" processes. Partisans of the former single out the nation state as the basic unit, or determining factor, in the yin and yang of world politics. The "macros," on the other hand, view world affairs on the lofty level of the civilizations to which nation-states belong and by which their behavior is allegedly largely determined. To one degree or another, much of the latter school's thinking, although they may be loath to admit it, derives from Oswald Spengler, Arnold Toynbee, Quincy Wright, F.N. Parkinson and others. In contrast, scholars such as Hans J. Morgenthau, John H. Herz and Raymond Aron have tended to hew to the "micro" school. Both schools began debating the issue vigorously back in the 1950s. That Huntington is resurrecting the controversy forty years later is symptomatic of the failure of globalism—specifically the idea of establishing a "new world order"—to take root and of the failure to make sense of contradictory trends and events. His aim is to find new, easily classified determinants of contemporary quasi-chaotic international behavior and thus to get a handle on the international kaleidoscope.

Huntington's methodology is not new. In arguing the macro case in the 1940s, Toynbee distinguished what he called primary, secondary and tertiary civilizations by the time of their appearance in history, contending that their attributes continued to influence contemporary events.

Wright, likewise applying an historical method, classified civilizations as "bellicose" (including Syrian, Japanese and Mexican), "moderately bellicose" (Germanic, Western, Russian, Scandinavian, etc.) and "most peaceful" (such as Irish, Indian, and Chinese). Like Toynbee and now Huntington, he attributed contemporary significance to these factors. Huntington's classification, while different in several important respects from those of his predecessors, also identifies determinants on a grand scale by "civilizations."

His endeavor, however, had its own fault lines. The real lines are the borders encompassing each distinct nation-state and mercilessly chopping the alleged civilizations into pieces. With the cultural and religious glue of these "civilizations" thin and cracked, with the nation-state's political regime providing the principal bonds, crisscross fracturing and cancellation of Huntington's own macro-scale, somewhat anachronistic fault lines are inevitable. The world thus remains fractured—mainly by nation-states—along political and possibly geopolitical lines. Allegedly deeply rooted cultural and historical determinants may be a great deal less vital and virulent than Huntington's and his many followers in Academe acknowledge—particularly among a number of the campus advocates of so-called "diversity" between whole regions. Undoubtedly, politics, regimes and ideologies are culturally, historically and "civilizationally" affected to an extent. Yet is it not the willful, day-to-day, crisis-to-crisis, war-to-war political decision making by sovereign nation-state units and their elites that remain the single most identifiable determinant of events in the international arena? How else can we explain the repeated nation-state "defections" from their collective "civilizations"? As Huntington himself points out in reference to the Persian Gulf War of 1990–91, "One Arab state invaded another and then fought a coalition of Arab, Western and other states."

For his part, veteran foreign affairs observer and thinker Raymond Aron described at length the primacy of a nation-state's political system, its inviolable territoriality, and sovereign impermeability. It is this that causes the plethora of differences in the polymorphic international arena, some of which cross and cancel Huntington's civilizations' fault lines. Aron observed that "men have believed that the fate of cultures was at stake on the battlefields at the same time as the fate of provinces." But, he added, the fact remains that sovereign states "are engaged in a competition for power [and] conquests. . . . In our times the major phenomenon [on the international scene] is the *heterogeneity of state units [not] supranational aggregations*" (my emphases).

What conclusions can we draw from the above canvas of the Huntingtonesque clash of civilizations within the context of the causation of cold wars? It appears that many scholars in cultural fields touching upon the diverse civilizations that Huntington identifies seem to agree that the so-called fault lines and divisions between said civilizations are extremely *permeable* to other influences besides their own or regional cultural traditions or "genes."

Thus, in the allegedly more or less monolithic, Confucian and Buddhist Orient, we see a radically divergent picture. A single descriptive label, such as "Confucian" or even "Southeast Asian" is not satisfactory. Take, for instance, the phenomenon of modern Singapore. Singapore is a unitary multiparty parliamentary republic that has a parliamentary government. Its political system is strikingly different from that of the neighboring People's Republic of China with its Soviet-derived, single-party structure that classifies it as a "party-state." Another example within the allegedly typical Oriental culture and civilization is the example of modern Japan. If by Huntington's standards and those of such writers as Karl von Wittfogel are any criteria, consider how far Japan with its liberal-democratic constitution has strayed from the expected "Oriental model." The same can be said of South Korea (ROK) and Taiwan (ROC). These nation-states "should not have" changed in the democratic ways they did after the 1960s—that is, if it is assumed they were valid members of the type of Oriental culture described by Wittfogel, Huntington, and others. Even Vietnam, though still ruled by a single Communist Party, shows signs of breaking through its fault line, especially in the way it conducts its foreign policy. India—which, admittedly, Huntington singled out as belonging to a separate branch of Oriental culture—is another leading case of the breakdown of the Huntington model when that model is applied axiomatically throughout a large region such as South Asia.

In their early Cold War, widely read book on the Russian political tradition, Carl Friedrich and Zbigniew Brzezinski described in *Totalitarian Dictatorship and Autocracy* the deeply imbedded "Oriental" tradition in Russia, including the Soviet period, in which old, traditional cultural determiners acted in ways that helped bring about Sovietism—and, in fact, the Cold War. After the collapse of the USSR and Communist rule in Russia and its non-Russian republics, it appeared that the Friedrich-Brzezinski model was proven false. For, after 1991, Russia, it seemed, had emerged from its Oriental-bureaucratic cocoon and was about to flourish as a democracy. As it turned out, this did not happen entirely as expected. So, the Friedrich-Brzezinski theory seemed to have been validated. Yet, enough political and social change nevertheless did occur in Russia that in the end, over a decade after the demise of the USSR the Russian Federation did not really resemble the Friedrich-Brzezinski model. It had fallen by the wayside. Observers of the Russian social and political scene today probably agree that even more sloughing off of traditional tsarist-*cum*-Soviet tradition lies ahead in the Russian future as democratization slowly proceeds. Instead, the specter of Russian history, rampant with autocracy and expansionism, seems to be abroad in the land.

The ultimate conclusion to be drawn from all this is that the U.S.-Soviet Cold War was not preordained or an inevitable product of civilization-clashing. Nor was the appearance of the Leninist-type party-state or Putinesque authoritarianism a foregone historical "necessity," whether in China, Russia, North Korea, or Cuba. Accidents, unforeseeable events, contingencies, and the emergence of particular, strong leaders and elites all contributed to a non-Soviet, non-ideological new Russia with a largely capitalist-type economy shorn of Soviet-style socialism. Russia's still bears some superficial resemblance to the tsarist and Soviet forebears. Yet the society is unique and, for some Russian observers, sufficiently dynamic and unpredictable as to avoid fitting into the Procrustean Bed of any single civilization model or, of course, being subject to any form of "historical determinism."

As to the relevance of this to the Cold War, some might naturally ask, Given a different, liberal-democratic system in Russia in the years preceding World War II and its postwar aftermath, would a cold war have arisen? This "metahistorical" question might be answered as follows: The East-West alliance in World War II would likely have been deep and lasting. The postwar era would not have seen the type of stand-off ideological clash and geostrategic rivalry that the Marxist-Leninist-Stalinist revolutionist dictatorship triggered. From this comes the inference that a nation's socio-political system definitely does influence its relations with other countries. Which seems obvious. Moreover, the deeply imbedded nature of the Marxist-Leninist-Stalinist political and social order and ideology were bound to produce East-West tensions. This was particularly true given Stalin's aggressive aims, above all, his anti-Western ideology and his abrasive tactics in inter-state relations with Western countries. These systemically embedded tactics continued after the dictator's death in March 1953.

This, in turn, suggests that any future cold war quite possibly will bear similar characteristics as the postwar Cold War if the confrontation is between a Communist-ruled state on one side *versus* a liberal-democratic state on the other. The conflict, say between the United States and Communist China, would likely depend on the nature of the social-political systems as they resemble those involved in the preceding U.S.-Soviet Cold War. Yet this should not be interpreted as an "historical necessity." For instance, a "cool peace" might take the place of an outright cold war. The prospect of a new cold war between China and the United States somewhat along lines of the old Cold War might best be described if coyly, as a probability. (A fuller discussion of this is reserved for chapter 6.)

NOTES

1. Quoted in George N. Crocker, *Roosevelt's Road to Russia*, Da Capo Press, N.Y., 1975, p. 249.

2. Quoted in Nisbet, op. cit., p. 77.

3. FDR remarked (Nisbet, op. cit., pp. 94–95): "[The Russian constitution's provisions concerning religion are] essentially what is the rule in this country [the U.S.]; only we don't put it the same way." Quoted in a number of sources, including Crocker, op. cit., p. 48. The idea that the USSR was changing and would eventually converge in some respects with America was believed by many of those Americans who uncritically sang the praises of the "gallant ally" of the East. Labor Secretary Frances Perkins wrote in her memoirs that she told FDR that she thought Russia now had the desire "to do the Holy Will." To which FDR responded: "You know, there may be something to that. It would explain their almost mystical devotion to the idea which they have developed of the Communist society. They all seem really to want to do what is good for their society instead of wanting to do only for themselves. We take care of ourselves and think about the welfare of society afterward."

4. "Law is the aggregate rules of conduct expressing the will of the dominant class and established by national assemblies (legislatures) as well as by customs and rules of the community as sanctioned by state power, the application of which is guarantee by the coercive force of the state for the purpose of guarding, strengthening, and developing the social relations and arrangements advantageous to and desired by the dominant class." Quoted in Julian Towster, *Political Power in the USSR, 1917–1947*, p. 8.

5. See Soviet, East German, ands Cuban Involvement in Fomenting Terrorism in Southern Africa, Committee on the Judiciary, U.S. Senate, November 1982. This U.S. government document describes overall Soviet Bloc support for Third World guerrilla and other types of "national-liberation" movements. For by far the most thoroughgoing book on all aspects of global terrorism, including those subsidized by the USSR, see Parry, op. cit.

6. "The Soviet Union had cast its veto 109 times by 1973, out of a total 128 vetoes used by the council." This exceeded several times over all vetoes cast by the five U.N. Permanent Members. http://en.wikipedia.org/wiki/Soviet_Union_and_the_United_Nations..

7. See Weeks, *Soviet and Communist Quotations* (New York: Pergamon-Brassey's, 1987), under "National and Global Hegemon," pp. 180–199.

SIX
Current Russian Texts on the Cold War

When the Soviet Union collapsed in 1991, it was necessary for Russians to begin thinking freely in un-Soviet ways. This was especially true of formal education rather than the former Soviet—or Maoist-style Marxist-Leninist indoctrination. Accordingly, it was urgent to write new history texts for the schools including secondary (high) schools and institutions of higher learning.

As a result of education reform, today every topic of Soviet history since 1917 is covered; viz., criticism of Marxist-Leninist ideology; surveys of Soviet foreign relations; domestic policy; Red Army military doctrine and strategy; the purges of the 'Thirties; the Nazi-Soviet pacts of 1939–40; the Winter War against Finland in late 1939; the cause of the Great Patriotic War on the eastern front, the Cold War—in fact, every major event that happened in the preceding seventy-four years of one-party Soviet rule. All this history had to be reexamined truthfully without ideological glosses and distorting propaganda of the past.

Here is the background for these revolutionary changes and the way they impact on various topics and events covered in the present book.

Educating children and young adults in the old, pre-1917 tsarist way, Lenin said, meant "cramming heads full of knowledge, 9/10ths of which was useless, 1/10th of which was distorted." According to the Bolsheviks, prior education in Russia was a big distraction meant to preserve the autocracy and inequality between classes. However, under Communism, Lenin claimed, students are indoctrinated in "socialism by its vanguard, the Communist Party, [in order to raise] a generation able to accomplish the final realization of full communism."

The "distortion" in education was thereupon updated by the new autocracy of party-state rule. For over two generations under Lenin, Stalin, and their successors, the teaching of Russian history and world history was deformed to fit the mold of Marxist-Leninist "science." Teachers were ordered to serve as "transmission belts" imparting to students the ideas of Communism and absolute loyalty to the self-perpetuating elitist regime. Describing the outside world as an "encirclement" of Soviet Russia and an "arena" of inevitable two-camp struggle between capitalism and socialism, school teachers at all levels were trained to be purveyors of class hatred and proponents of class struggle against bourgeois enemies at home and abroad. They were also to describe the USSR as the "citadel of socialism," the model for all other countries in the world.

Soon other elements were added into the Soviet curriculum as well as indoctrination of the masses in or out of school. These methods became totalitarian prototypes that were deliberately and admittedly copied by the Nazis as well as by other one-party dictatorships of the Communist type.

Fortunately, with the demise of Communist rule in Russia in 1991 and the end of the Cold War, the country's education system was purged of some but not all such *"partiinost,* "Communist content, methods, and Soviet slant. Most significantly, Russian students today are no longer forced to read textbooks whose chapters are slanted according to one-party ideology imbued with "class-consciousness," "global struggle for socialism," and adulation of The Leader, whether living or dead.

So, then, what are Tolya and Tatyana reading today as they do their homework for their history classes? How are their education and textbooks different from those of Soviet days? What light do the new history textbooks throw on the Cold War?

POST-SOVIET TEXTBOOKS

Two representative textbooks used in today's classes in Russia illustrate the sea-change that has occurred in latter-day Russian education. The books are designed for 10th and 11th graders. Some are recommended by the RF Ministry of Education, but are not necessarily adopted obligatorily. Some schools in today's Russia are private. Public school administrations also enjoy latitude in selection of textbooks.

Two new texts, titled *The World in the 20th Century* and *A History of Russia*, are accompanied by "apparatus"—for example, "Questions for Discussion," designed to stimulate what the authors call "free, open discussion" in the classroom. Indeed, the questions in these textbooks are mostly thought-provoking and well-intended in the pursuit of discussion. Each chapter includes fragments of primary-source material, some of which would be edifying even for readers of Western Soviet histories; tables of governmental institutions under the tsars and Soviets; the post-

1991 quasi-democratic government structure of the Russian Federation, and so on.

One of the pair of books includes a glossary while both contain a chronology as well as maps. The glossary is noteworthy for its totally non-ideological definitions. This strikes contrast with the glossaries found in the texts of the Soviet period right up until 1991.[1] The latter provided only "politically-correct" definitions designed for the uncritical student. These definitions were incorporated in the well-known Soviet "Political Dictionaries:" that provided strict party-line definitions of socio-political terms for civilians as well as the military. In international affairs, the editorialized handling of topics in Soviet times were predictable, especially as concerned the Cold War: the Cuban Missile Crisis; the U.S.-USSR arms buildup; the nuclear stand-off; the Soviet-led invasion of Czechoslovakia in August 1968 under the "Brezhnev Doctrine"; "détente"; the Soviet invasion of Afghanistan in December 1979, and so on.

In informal interviews conducted by this writer of Russian high-school and college-age students in the 1990s, it became clear to me that their reading of post-Communist texts in the RF had created a generational "time warp" of knowledge about their own country and the world in comparison to previous generations of Russian students, whom I had talked with in the USSR in 1966. One senses that today's Russian students have experienced shock in learning of the grimness and hypocrisy of the Soviet past, including the period of the Cold War. This is not to say that millions of post-Soviet graduates from post-Soviet school entirely agree on all aspects of the Cold War, especially its origin and causes, and "who started it."

Russia's totalitarian system up to 1991 treated historiography as a Communist Party tool. As in Maoist and post-Maoist China, the one-party leadership considered the rendering of history to be one of the highest political functions of the party-state, and the party leadership. Controlling the depiction of the historical past was for the Communist leaders, as it is today in Beijing, the preserve of the political leadership,. not of scholars alone. With the result that the Soviets severely censored history texts for the duration of Soviet rule. As in China today, Soviet scholars, represented via the Academy of Sciences, were expected under duress not to allow breaches of party discipline. To make sure, the party placed overseers in academic institutions while supervising publishing houses newspapers, broadcasting, and the cinema.[2]

Throughout the Soviet period up to 1991, the interpretation of the Cold War in Soviet history texts embodied the predictable Communist Party line. Namely, that

- America initiated the Cold War because of its inveterate, "systemic" bourgeois capitalist-imperialist interest in encircling and ulti-

mately destroying Soviet power since the USSR represented a revolutionary danger to Western bourgeois democracy.
- While the Roosevelt Administration, until the president's death on April 12, 1945, was no less imperialist than any other Washington leadership, Franklin D. Roosevelt himself, nevertheless, was relatively amenable to the demands put to him by Stalin, demands that amounted to purely "defencist" policies to ensure that the borderlands—that is, the half-dozen neighboring countries bordering the USSR to the west—would not be hostile to the Soviet Union as the east European region was 1939–41 to the eve of the German invasion of June 22, 1941. The new Truman Administration, it is claimed, became overtly hostile to the USSR. Unlike the preceding Roosevelt Administration, Truman's fell more under the sway of "reactionary, imperialist elements" in Wall Street. These elements, in turn, favored aggressive, military resolution of the bilateral differences with the USSR based on American preponderance of power. President Truman's new "hard line" was marked by ex-Prime Minister Winston Churchill's "iron curtain" speech in Fulton, MO, in March 1946. With justification, it is alleged, Stalin reacted strongly to the speech in his *Pravda* statement later that month.
- For its part, Soviet foreign policy under Stalin and his successors to 1991 pursued a policy of "peaceful coexistence" with the "capitalist encirclement," led by the United States. This encirclement was deemed in portions of Soviet military and civilian literature to be the work of the "main enemy," the United States.

OTHER POST-SOVIET BOOKS

The above two types of "liberalized" textbooks by no means dominate the field. In fact, it is probably more accurate to say that the textbooks that deviate radically from the former Soviet model tend to be the exception rather than the rule in the post-Soviet RF. Others reflect polls taken in recent years on Stalin's posthumous popularity in the RF. It is estimated that today almost half, perhaps more than half, of the Russian population regards Stalin having been a "great" leader who saved the country against destruction by the Nazis. A variety of other interpretations as concerns the topic of Stalin's rule, foreign policy, and the Cold War show any number of variations in the most recent books published in the RF.

- One species of textbook and volume for the general reader adopts the line that Stalin, although he made mistakes and at times applied exaggerated brutality, was "great" for having saved the Russian state from annihilation in the Second World War.[3]
- Another group of recent books claims that Stalin's record has been sullied not only by "Anglo-Saxon" propaganda but by the Khrush-

chev campaign begun in 1956 to disown and scorn Stalin. These books call Khrushchev an "inveterate liar" who helped sap the very existence of the USSR and Sovietism.[4]
- Another species of history text, which appears to win only limited sympathy among Russian readers, takes a radically anti-Stalin view. Such books claim that not only did Stalin plan a preemptive war against Germany in 1941 (getting the jump on a German Wehrmacht attack of June 22), but was planning a postwar World War III against the capitalist world.
- Some post-Soviet books are simply bizarre. One, by Nikolai Starikov, titled *Stalin: The Way We Remember Him* (Piter Press, St. Petersburg, 2013), goes so far as to allege (p. 129), that "Adolf Hitler was egged on to start a war with Russia [sic].

In general, it can be said that post-Soviet Russia has some distance to go before it recognizes--officially and objectively in its published literature--how Stalin and his regime bore the main responsibility for unleashing the Cold War. It appears that some resistance by Russian authors in taking the step toward non-ideological objectivity is the manner in which Stalin's Russia-centered policies under Putin tends to jibe with those of the post-Stalin leadership.

Stripped of Communist ideology as they were after the demise of the Soviet Union, the foreign policies of Stalin and his successors certainly included a number of typically Russian-national drivers. These factors not only go back to early expansionist/revolutionary Soviet Russia under Lenin. They reflect tsarist policies of the past. Russian rulers characteristically, jealously, and determinedly guard their over-extended frontiers, west to east. The gradual encroachments today that some Western and Russian authors see stemming from the rise of post-Mao China and its ambitions (now confined to large-scale trade) with respect to the five former states of Soviet-ruled Central Asia, which are over-the-mountains neighbors of the PRC—Kazakhstan, Uzbekistan, Kyrgyzstan, Tadzhikistan, and Turkmenistan—are reminders of how conscious the Kremlin is of its once territorial integrity—that, indeed, reverts to times of Peter the Great, Catherine the Great, and Russia's expanded influence into the Balkans and Far East in the nineteenth century.

That this former influence is slipping out of Moscow's grasp is obviously of concern to Russia's present leaders. They are attempting under President Putin, in fact, to create their own Euro-Asian bloc that includes these resource-rich, former Soviet possessions of Central Asia.

At present there are no definite signs of an emerging cold war with Communist China over the increasing Chinese influence in this large, resource-rich, former region of Soviet control. The violent Sino-Russian cold war fought over frontiers along Amur River in the Far East in the 1960s has been "officially forgotten." The emphasis today in Sino-Russian relations is on trade and a degree of "strategic partnership." This includes fighting what Beijing and Moscow have agreed mutually to label, "U.S. global hegemonism."

NOTES

1. As to glossaries, take for instance the following ideology-free definition of "parliamentarism" found in one post-Soviet history text:

> It is system of governmental rule in which the functions of the legislature are executive are strictly delimited and in which the parliament plays the leading role in the system. In this system, the parliament is viewed as both subject and object within the political struggle and is linked to traditional democratic values in the country.

Contrast this to the 1987 definition of political democracy with that found in the 1988 encyclopedic dictionary, titled "The Contemporary United States of America," edited by ideologists including, ironically, the Russian interim prime minister in the Yeltsin post-Soviet period, Yevgeny Primakov:

> The most important aspect of the American political system is the two-party rule [which is] an instrument for retaining political domination by the monopolistic bourgeoisie.

Or compared to this definition of Western democracy once made by Lenin, which cropped up in many texts in the Soviet period:

> "Capital dominates and stifles everything [and] this what they call democracy.

2. On how this control is accomplished in the PRC, see a thoroughgoing study: Anne-Marie Brady, *Marketing Dictatorship: Propaganda and Thought Work in Contemporary China* (Lanham, MD: Rowman and Littlefield, 2008).

3. See Albert L. Weeks, *Assured Victory*, Chapter 1, for examples of this interpretation of Stalin's "greatness." This strain has cropped up in public speeches, including those of Presidents Vladimir Putin and Dmitri Medvedev (ibid, pp. xxii–xxiv).

4. A prime example of this trend is Arsen Martirosyan, *Stalin: Biografiya Vozhdya (Stalin: Biography of the Leader)* (Moscow: Veche, 2008), which is one of over six other titles under Martirosyan's authorship. His *Stalin After the War, 1943–1953* asserts that the Cold War was the West's doing. It was aimed, he wrote, at destroying the USSR. Helping in this process, he claims, were Moscow's own feckless leaders and outright shams, like Nikita Khrushchev. Martirosyan and other authors of his type (viz., Valdimir Petrov; Yu. Zhukov; Ye. A. Prudniklova; A.I. Koplakidi; A. Bushkova; M. Kalashnikov; S. Mironin et al.) show an anti-Semitic bias that is popular among some Russian readers. These writers insist that Khrushchev himself was a species of "Trotskyite" who was in the pay of Anglo-Saxon and Masonic financial circles in the West. All such books focus on Churchill's Fulton, MO, "iron curtain" speech of March 1946 as the symbolic opening shot in the Cold War initiated by the West. No one of these books (in resembling in this respect some of those in the West) ever cites the belligerent electoral speeches made in February 1946 by Stalin and Molotov. Which in fact can be regarded as signaling the beginning of the Cold War, in this case by the same two, top leaders of the Soviet Union. By contrast, Churchill was not in power in London when he made his speech in Missouri. Moreover, the U.S. Government gave no official support for the ex-Prime Minister's speech. That year, 1946, the OWI issued its pro-Soviet handbook for U.S. armed service personnel (see Appendix I). Churchill's blunt speech unnerved many U.S. columnists (like Walter Lippmann) and newspaper editorial writers, who found Churchill's remarks to be unreasonably "anti-Soviet." Others

in the U.S. Government also disclaimed support for Churchill's speech. Numerous Western Cold War authors still single out Churchill's address as sounding the death knell of the World War II "grand" or "strange" alliance. They thus ignore the earlier Soviet speeches as well as abundant anti-West Soviet ideology and propaganda that early amounted to "declarations" of cold war. Stalin's at times bitter, accusatory correspondence with Churchill and Roosevelt in 1943 (over Soviet insistence to immediately open a Second Front in the West or Soviet claims that the Western powers were making a separate peace with Nazi Germany). Stalin's agitation over a second front was motivated in part by his fear that Churchill's plan might be carried out for an invasion into Eastern Europe. This would have frustrated Soviet plans to occupy and sovietize that region. Thus Stalin insisted on a distant, cross-Channel invasion from England to France rather than an attack on the "soft underbelly" of eastern Europe and southern France that would probably have been easier for the Allies to have executed than that of assaulting Normandy across over thirty-five miles of sea and which faced a heavily defended coastline by some of Hitler's best armies. The effort on the French coast was commanded by the "Desert Fox," Field Marshal Erwin Rommel.

Appendix 1
Myths of the Cold War
Albert L. Weeks

AMERICA'S "DEMOCRATIC" ALLY

What GIs Were Told About Stalin and Soviet Russia

The year 1949 marked the sixtieth anniversary of a major turning point in relations between America and the USSR. That year saw the formation of a postwar alliance between Stalin and Mao (who had just founded the People's Republic of China) that led by a red thread to the brutal Korean War. This was the beginning of an intensified U.S.-Soviet Cold War that was accompanied by very hot "proxy wars" supported by the Soviets and their allies worldwide.

Yet just a few years before this, the United States and the USSR had been comrades in the war against the Axis. Soviet Russia became an ally of the Western Powers in World War II shortly after the Nazi armies poured into the USSR on June 22, 1941. The invaluable Lend-Lease soon followed, Marshal Georgy Zhukov, the "Soviet Eisenhower," later admitting that this U.S. aid had "saved" the USSR.

During the war, a lot of friendly talk about "Uncle Joe" Stalin and our "gallant" and "democratic" ally in the East was bandied about by our Government for the consumption of our GI's. The reputation of this new, Soviet team member of the democratic alliance was whitewashed by our Office of War Information (OWI). As thus presented to U.S. Army Orientation Officers, GI's were given a totally misleading view of Stalin's dictatorship and what Russian novelist Alexander Solzhenitsyn called the "socialist labor camp (Gulag) on a national scale."

Most soldiers at that time understood that the "enemy of my enemy is my friend." But beyond that truism, the U.S. Army's college-educated orientation officers had their work cut out for them in attempting to depict the Soviets as something more than just an ally-of-convenience and, instead, as a true, lasting friend and collaborator in the postwar world. Yet the Army and OWI set out to do just that: to present Stalin's Russia as a democratic country deserving of respect and admiration. Meanwhile, all the evil deeds perpetrated by Lenin and Stalin since 1917—the Gulag labor camps, the bloody purges, the millions of victims of Stalin's collectivization drive and deliberate starvation policies, the utter lack of democracy—would all be overlooked.

In contrast to our friendly campaigns, Soviet propaganda never accepted the Western Allies as true friends. In Moscow, the USSR's alliance with us and the West was called simply a "coalition," a demeaning term. Moreover, suspicion was cast by the Soviets on the Western Allies' strategy and tactics in the war. A bad impression of the Western Allies was given Soviet citizens by their government not only over the "delayed" opening of a second front in the West. Soviet propaganda during the war never ceased hurling epithets like "imperialist," "bourgeois," "monopoly capitalists, " et al., at America, Britain, France and the other Allies. (Of course, during the Nazi-Soviet honeymoon alliance of August 1939 to June 1941, the Nazis and the Soviet Communists collaborated in making such attacks against the democratic West as Stalin materially helped the German armies defeat France, Norway, and the Lowland countries.)

In contrast to this, OWI and U.S. Army orientation officers heaped praise upon the Soviet system, the leader, Stalin, and their (allegedly) egalitarian socialism. Myth-making about Soviet Russia really got out of hand (I remember as a USAF officer in WW II reading one of these pieces of OWI propaganda). American soldiers became *dis*oriented rather than honestly "oriented" about the Soviets.

A few excerpts from the War Department's *Brief Handbook for the Use of Officers of the Armed Forces of the United States* titled, "The USSR Institutions and People" (in a 1945 edition), suffice to illustrate this disormation about Stalin's Russia. To wit:

Soviet "freedom," "democracy," and socialism:

"[Subtitle] Democracy in the USSR. . . . The Soviet Constitution also provides, as has been indicated, for a representative government, elected by secret ballot on the basis of universal, direct and equal suffrage." (p. 40)

"The Soviets place great emphasis . . . on economic security as the basis of individual freedom, and Stalin once said that 'there is real freedom only when exploitation has been destroyed.'" (Ibid.)

"The Soviet citizen has a number of economic rights. His wages may be spent as he pleases, subject to payment of income and other taxes. He may save money, depositing it in a savings bank or buying government bonds and drawing interest thereon. He owns his clothing, his household utensils, his phonograph, and other personal effects. . . . He may also use a small plot of land to raise food for himself and his family, and if he has a small surplus of food he may sell it personally to others. . . . The Soviet government frowns upon the accumulation of personal fortunes." (p. 32)

"The status of religion has improved markedly. . . . Besides providing freedom of conscience, the [Stalin] Constitution also allows freedom of anti-religious propaganda. . . . The government has revealed a tolerant attitude toward organized religion." (p. 41)

"Mass participation [in politics] is encouraged as an indication of public will, and particularly as a check on bureaucratic tendencies . . ." (Ibid.)

"Individual competitive enterprise is considered pregnant with conflict, wasteful and destructive. [The people] are told that this type of government alone makes it possible to establish wisely, and to work successfully toward, definite social, economic, and political goals for the benefit of the nation as a whole." (p. 43)

The Soviet population; the Russian people; how all Soviet peoples are like Russians:
"The population of the USSR is characterized not only by its absolute strength, but by the vigor of its growth or natural increase." (p. 14) (N.B.: This blatantly false statement in the pamphlet deserves comment. The Soviet population was severely diminished by a toll of at least 30 million people of various nationalities because of oppression and genocide after 1917 under Lenin and Stalin. As post-Communist demographers have shown, these policies sharply decreased the "natural" growth in population. The war toll alone amounted to at least 27 million lives, a large portion of whom fell as unfortunate victims of Stalin's mistakes in the war, his incarceration and liquidation within the Soviet Army and among civilians of "cowards" and "deserters," and other forms of oppression and genocide perpetrated against individuals and whole nations under Soviet sway.)

"The United States is the only country in the Western Hemisphere which can be compared with the Soviet Union in regard to the national diversity of the people who compose its population. [The USSR] is a multi-national state composed of constitutionally equal peoples. [They] are encouraged to preserve and develop their national traditions, cultures, and languages." (pp. 19–20)

"Many of the personal attributes of Russians are displayed by members of the other nationalities of the USSR, and those particular personality patterns which are fostered by life under the Soviet regime will appear in [the] Russian and non-Russian alike."

Appendix II
Molotov's and Stalin's Electoral Speeches

[Emphases mine—ALW]

ELECTORAL SPEECH BY V. M. MOLOTOV, FEBRUARY 6, 1946

Comrades!

... Permit me to express my deep gratitude for the confidence you have accorded thereby to the Communist Party, for the confidence and honor you have accorded me personally as a representative of the Party. I thank you for the kind words you have said here about me and my work. On my part I wish to assure you and all the electors that I remember well what Comrade Stalin said about a Deputy's prime duty: to have the great image of great Lenin before him and to emulate Lenin in everything. To emulate Lenin means at the same time to emulate great Stalin, the continuer of Lenin's cause. There can be no nobler task for a Deputy than to emulate Lenin and Stalin and to be worthy of this in fact. Rest assured, Comrade electors, that I shall always and with all my heart strive toward this goal.

Test of Leadership

We are on the eve of new general elections. The entire adult population of the country is taking part in these elections. The attitude of all the many millions in the Soviet Union toward the leadership of the Communist Party and toward the policy of the Soviet Government is now being put to the test. Well, we have reason to look confidently ahead. Proof of this is also supplied by the fact that the bloc of Communists and non-

Party people has gained still greater strength and pursues its work with concerted efforts.

Perhaps some persons abroad still dream that it would be a good thing if some other party, not the Communist Party, were to assume the leadership of our country. To these persons one could reply with a simple proverb: "from another world." As for our people, they have their own opinion on the subject. How can it be helped if the Soviet people have formed bonds of close kinship with their Communist Party? And if some persons abroad still do not like it, we can console them: in other countries, too, it is no rare thing nowadays to find that the Communists as leaders enjoy the confidence of the broad masses of the people. This only goes to show that the lessons taught by life are not in vain. So the earth does not merely go round; we may say that it does not go round for nothing and that it is pursuing its course forward to a better future.

Four years of war with Germany and later with Japan was the supreme test for the young Soviet State. This war, which placed a strain on all the spiritual and material forces of the nation, was an exceptionally grave test of the policy of the Bolshevik Party. More than that, it was a test of the stability of the very state system of the Soviet Republic. Now no one can deny that the Soviet State has passed this test with flying colors.

Comparison with Past

Compare Russia before the October Revolution with what the Soviet Union is now. It is a well known fact that the Russo-Japanese War of 1904–1905 caused an upheaval in tsarist Russia. Everyone remembers the first Russian revolution when the first thunderbolt burst over tsarism. The war with Germany in 1914–1917 undermined tsarism at its roots and ended with the abolition of the bourgeois landowners' regime in Russia.

At the time of the war with Japan, the tsarist government hastened to end the war, admitting its defeat. In the war with Germany, tsarist Russia was not able to survive, demonstrating how utterly rotten and obsolete the old regime was.

Compare this with the present position of our country after the most difficult war with Germany and then a war with Japan as well. Both aggressors, together with their satellites, have been routed, chiefly owing to our Red Army.

The Soviet Union achieved victory in the West and then in the East as well, which as you see is quite unlike the old pre-Soviet times. Having passed these supreme tests, the Soviet Union has made still greater advance as a major factor in international life. The USSR ranks today among the world powers, enjoying the highest prestige. Important problems of international relations cannot now be settled without the participation of the Soviet Union or without heeding the voice of our homeland. The participation of Comrade Stalin is regarded as the best guarantee of a successful solution of complicated international problems.

New Position

Without indulging in self-complacency, always remembering how stubbornly reactionary forces still cling to life in capitalist countries, we must, nevertheless, recognize that the new position the Soviet Union now occupies in international relations is not the result of some fortuitous circumstance, that it meets the interests of all peace-loving nations and also the interests of all countries advancing along the road of democratic development and assertion of their national independence.

Credit for all this goes primarily to the heroic Red Army. Our Red Army and Red Navy men, officers, commanders, all services, have given the most devoted service for the glory of our Motherland. Our Generals and Marshals, with Generalissimo Stalin at their head, have brought the Soviet Union glory and renown. The enemy was checked at the gates of Moscow, and this was the beginning in the turn of the tide of the Soviet-German front. The enemy surrounded Leningrad but proved powerless to carry out his plan of capturing that city. The enemy was routed at Stalingrad, and from then on the utter rout of the German army began on our front. These tasks were accomplished on a strategic plan and under the immediate guidance of Comrade Stalin, our great Army leader.

The defeat of the enemy came as a result of the efforts of the entire Soviet people who ensued the victory. We had to lengthen the working day. Millions of women replaced men on the collective farms, at the factories and plants. Youths self-sacrificingly did the work of adults. We had to reconcile ourselves to serious restrictions in supply of the most vital necessities, to grave housing shortage, to evacuation to distant parts and to other wartime hardships. And in spite of this our national economy has coped with its main tasks. The needs of the front were satisfied without fail or delay. The urgent needs of the rear were also met, although with great restrictions. Comrade Stalin's call, "Everything for the front!" was unanimously taken up by the entire Soviet people and this ensured victory.

We arrived at victory having overcome all the difficulties at the front and in the rear. We were able to do this because not only during the war, but in the years preceding it, we followed the correct path. We swept from our road internal enemies, all those saboteurs and subversive elements who in the end turned into a gang of spies and wreckers in the employ of foreign masters. It is also known that the Soviet people have long checked any ambition for direct foreign intervention into our internal affairs. In spite of all those who put spokes in our wheel, our people transformed their country and created a mighty socialist state.

The foundations of our victory were laid by the creation of the Red Army, industrialization of the country, reconstruction of agriculture on the basis of collective farming, intensive work for raising the cultural level of the population, and the persistent training of engineering and other skilled personnel. And now we are able to sum up the splendid results: we have routed a most dangerous enemy, scored a glorious victory, rallied the family of Soviet peoples still closer, and raised the international prestige of the Soviet Union to unprecedented heights. What better test could there be of the correctness of the policy of the Bolshevik Party? After this, it is not difficult to understand why the confidence in our Party has grown so much, why the confidence in Comrade Stalin's leadership is so unshakable.

New Tasks

The termination of the war confronted us with new tasks, imposing also new obligations upon us. The time has come to set about the work interrupted by the war. We shall need some time to raise socialist industry to the level it had reached before the war. But in a couple of years we shall accomplish it, which is more than any capitalist country could do. This task will be an integral part of the new Five-Year Plan which we are launching this year and which in many respects will enable us to surpass our prewar level of economic development. We are again developing branches of industry which will provide agriculture with tractors, farm machinery and fertilizer in the amounts it needs, and also those industries which will furnish locomotives, rolling stock and everything else needed for railways and other important forms of transportation, sea and river shipping and automobile traffic. Another task on the order of the day is an all-round improvement in the supply of consumer goods for the population of town and country. For that a number of our industries will have to be expanded. The problem of overcoming the housing shortage is particularly acute now in view of the ravages which the war against the German invader has left behind it. We must raise to proper standard the construction of schools and hospitals, institutes and laboratories, cinemas and theaters and many other cultural and social institutions everywhere, taking account of the shortcomings in the past and of the need to draw more extensively on the experience of other countries. The people of Moscow will again take up plans for the reconstruction of the Capital, and all of us will actively participate in this major state undertaking.

Main Task

You will remember that shortly before the war the Party and the Government acknowledged that the time had come to undertake and accomplish in practice the main economic task of the USSR. This main task was formulated as follows: to overtake and surpass economical the most highly developed capitalist European countries and the United States of America, and to accomplish this task fully in the nearest future. Our country must produce no less industrial goods per capita of the population than the most developed capitalist country-that is the task.

We launched this work successfully. But Germany's attack interrupted the great work we had begun. Now we shall take it up anew with still more profound realization of its importance, and we shall try to make the pace of our work commensurate with the greatness of this task. We do not know and shall not know crises when industry slumps, as is the case in capitalist countries. We do not and shall not know unemployment, for we have long discarded the fetters of capitalism and the rule of private property. Conscious endeavor and socialist emulation in our factories and mills, on collective and State farms, on railways and in the offices are bringing us economic progress.

We must especially strive to make the labor of each worker more productive, for that is not only in the personal interest of every working man and woman, but in the common interest of the State. The time has passed when work was done to the strains of "Dubinushka." Of course "Dubinushka" is a good song and is the song of the Volga boatmen. But there is a proper time for everything.

In our age, the age of machinery and highly-developed technology, and especially when we are out to "overtake and surpass" . . .

STALIN'S ELECTION SPEECH, FEBRUARY 9, 1946

[U.S. Supreme Court Associate Justice William O. Douglas called this speech by Stalin a "declaration of World War II."[1]

Comrades! Eight years have elapsed since the last elections. This is a period rich in events of a decisive character. The first four years passed in strenuous work of the Soviet people in the fulfillment of the Third Five-Year Plan. During the past four years the events of the struggle against the German and Japanese aggressors developed events of the Second World War. Doubtless the war was the main event of that period.

It would be incorrect to think that the war arose accidentally or as the result of the fault of some of the statesmen. Although these faults did exist, the war arose in reality as the inevitable result of the development of the world economic and political forces on the basis of monopoly capitalism.

Our Marxists declare that the capitalist system of world economy conceals elements of crisis and war, that the development of world capitalism does not follow a steady and even course forward, but proceeds through crises and catastrophes. The uneven development of the capitalist countries leads in time to sharp disturbances in their relations, and the group of countries which consider themselves inadequately provided with raw materials and export markets try usually to change this situation and to change the position in their favor by means of armed force. As a result of these factors, the capitalist world is sent into two hostile camps and war follows.

Perhaps the catastrophe of war could have been avoided if the possibility of periodic redistribution of raw materials and markets between the countries existed in accordance with their economic needs, in the way of coordinated and peaceful decisions. But this is impossible under the present capitalist development of world economy.

Thus, as a result of the first crisis in the development of the capitalist world economy, the First World War arose. The Second World War arose as a result of the second crisis. . . .

What about the origin and character of the Second World War? In my opinion, everybody now recognizes that the war against fascism was not, nor could it be, an accident in the life of the people; that the war turned into a war of the peoples for their existence; that precisely for this reason it could not be a speedy war, a "lightning war." As far as our country is concerned, this war was the most cruel and hard of all wars ever experienced in the history of our motherland. But the war has not only been a curse; it was at the same time a hard school of trial and a testing of all the people's forces. . . .

And so, what is the balance of the war; what are our conclusions? . . .

Now victory means, first of all, that our Soviet social system has won, that the Soviet social system has successfully stood the test in the fire of war and has proved its complete vitality. . . .

The war has shown that the Soviet multi-national state system has successfully stood the test, has grown still stronger during the war and has proved a completely vital state system. . . .

Third, our victory implies that it was the Soviet armed forces that won. Our Red Army had won. The Red Army heroically withstood all the adversities of the war, routed completely the armies of our enemies and emerged victoriously from the war. . . .

Now a few words on the plans for the work of the Communist Party in the near future. As is known, these plans are confirmed in the very near future. The fundamental task of the new Five-Year Plan consists in restoring the areas of the country which have suffered, restoring the prewar level in industry and agriculture, and then exceeding this level by more or less considerable amounts. . . . [Stalin then goes on to emphasize defense—related production of heavy industry and like Molotov, predicts achievement of Soviet supremacy over the U.S. Emphases mine.—ALW.]

1. See http://www.skwirk.com/p-c_s-56_u-490_t-1333_c-5122/tas/sose-history/australia-after-1945/the-spread-of-communism-after-world-war-ii/communism-after-1945-background]

Appendix III

Soviet Communist Party Secretary Andrei Zhdanov's "Two-Camp" Cold War Speech, January 16, 1948

[N.B.: Cf. *U.S. News-World Report*, 16 January 1948, pp. 68–71. "Section 3a: Cold War Launched. . . . The Russian Government has committed itself to defeating the Marshall Plan for aiding Western Europe. It intends to use communist parties everywhere to attain that goal. The strategy for developing and carrying out the Soviet campaign is made clear in a talk by Andrei Zhdanov, a member of the Politburo that rules Russia, and one of the five most influential officials in the U.S.S.R. Government. The following is from a speech Mr. Zhdanov delivered in Poland, in September 1947, before a meeting of the Communist parties of nine European countries."]

"American imperialism seek . . . to utilize the postwar difficulties of the European countries, in particular, the shortage of raw materials, fuel and food in the Allied countries which most in the war, for the purpose of dictating to them slavish conditions of aid.

"Anticipating an impending economic crisis, the U.S.A. is making haste to find new monopoly spheres for the investment of capital and for markets. U.S. economic 'aid' pursues the broad purpose of enslaving Europe by American capital. The graver the economic condition of one country or another, the harsher the terms which the American monopolies seek to dictate. But economic control involves also the political subordination to American imperialism.

"American monopolies, 'rescuing' one country or another from famine and chaos, seek to deprive that country of any independence. American 'aid' almost automatically involves a change in the political policy of the country to which this 'aid' is extended . . .

"Finally, the desire for world domination and an antidemocratic policy on the part of the U.S.A. includes ideological warfare. The fundamental task of the ideological part of the American strategic plan lies in blackmailing public opinion, disseminating slander regarding the imaginary aggressiveness of the Soviet Union and the countries of the new democracy, and thereby presenting the Anglo-Saxon bloc in the role of the defending side and removing from it responsibility for preparing a fresh war.

During the second World War, the popularity of the Soviet Union grew tremendously abroad. Through its self-sacrificing and heroic struggle against imperialism, the Soviet Union won the love and respect of working people in all countries . . .

"In the ideological struggle against the USSR, the American imperialists, demonstrating their ignorance, put forward first of all the idea of portraying the Soviet Union as a force alleged to be undemocratic and totalitarian, and the U.S.A., Britain and the entire capitalist world as democracy. . . . A specific expression of the expansionist aspirations of the U.S.A. under present conditions is to be found in the Truman Doctrine as well as the Marshall Plan. . . . The Truman Doctrine, which seeks to offer American assistance to all reactionary regimes actively fighting against democratic peoples is of a frankly aggressive nature. Its publication elicited certain embarrassment even in circles of American capitalists who are used to anything. Progressive public elements in the U.S.A. and in other countries resolutely protested against the challenging, frankly imperialist nature of Truman's act.

"The unfavorable reception which greeted the Truman Doctrine elicited the need for the Marshall Plan, which is a more veiled attempt at carrying through one and the same expansionist policy.

"The essence of the hazy, deliberately camouflaged formulae of the Marshall Plan lies in cementing a bloc of states connected by their obligations to the U.S.A. and in offering American credits in payment for repudiation by the European states of their economic and, subsequently, their political independence.

"The basis of the Marshall Plan lies in the restoration of the industrial areas of Western Germany under the control of American monopolies. . . . The Soviet Government has never objected to the use of foreign and, particularly, American credits, as a means capable of accelerating the process of economic reconstruction. However, the Soviet Union has always proceeded from the fact that the credit terms should not be of an enslaving nature, and should not lead to the economic and political enslavement of the debtor state to the creditor state.

"Proceeding from this same political principle, the Soviet Union has always defended the position that foreign credits should not be the principal means of the restoration of a country's economy. The fundamental and decisive condition for economic reconstruction should be the use of internal forces and resources of any country and the creation of its own industry. . . . The Soviet Union constantly defends the thesis that political and economic relations among various states should be founded exclusively on the principle of equality of the parties and mutual respect for their sovereign rights. . . . The Communists must be the leading force in co-opting all anti-Fascist freedom-loving elements in the struggle against the new American expansionist plans for the enslaving of Europe.

"It must be kept in mind that there is a tremendous difference between the desire of the imperialists to unleash a new war and the possibility of organizing such a war. The peoples of the world do not want a war . . ."

Bibliography

Afanas'iev, Yu. N. (ed). *Drugaya voina (The Other War)*. Moscow: Rossiiskii Gosudarstvenniy Universitet, 1996.
Alperovitz, Gar. *Atomic Diplomacy: Hiroshima and Potsdam*. New York: Penguin Press, 1985.
Andrew, Christopher and Mitrokhin, Vasili. *The Sword and the Shield: The Mitrokhin Archive and the Secret History of the KGB*. New York: Basic Books, 1999.
Anisimov, Yevgeniy. *Istoriya Rossii ot Riurika do Putina, lyudi, sobytiya, daty (History of Russia from Riurik to Putin: People, Events, Dates)*. St. Petersburg: Piter Press, 2008
Antonov-Ovseyenko, A. *Portret tirana (Portrait of a Tyrant)*. Moscow: Peidg, 1994.
———. *The Time of Stalin: Portrait of Tyranny*. New York: Harper and Row, 1980.
Applebaum, Anne. *Iron Curtain: The Crushing of Eastern Europe, 1944–1956*. New York: Penguin Books, 2012
Azovstev, N. N. *V. I. Lenin i sovetskaya voyennaya nauka (V. I. Lenin and Soviet Military Science)*. Moscow: Nauka, 1981.
Bagdararyan, B. E et al. *Shkol'niy uchebnik istorii i gosudarstvennaya politika (School Textbook on History and State Policy)*. Moscow: Nauchniy Ekspert, 2009.
Baldwin, Hanson W. *The Crucial Years 1939–1941: The World at War*. New York: Harper and Row Publishers, 1970.
Barsenkov, A. S. and Vdovin, A. I. *Istoriya Rossii, 1917–2009: Uchebnoye Posobiye (History of Russia, 1917–2009: School Textbook)*. Moscow: Aspekt Press, 2010
Basistov, Yu. V. *Stalin—Gitler: Ot Pakta do Voiny (Stalin and Hitler: From the Pact to War)*. St. Petersburg: Blitz Publishers, 2001.
Becker, Fritz. *Stalins Blutspur durch Europa: Partner des Westens 1933–45 (Stalin's Bloody Tracks Across Europe: The West's Partner 1933–45)*. Kiel, Germany: Arndt, 1995.
Bellamy, Chris. *Absolute War: Soviet Russia in the Second World War*. New York: Alfred A. Knopf, 2007.
Beloff, Max. *The Foreign Policy of Soviet Russia*. New York: Oxford University Press, 1953.
Berezhkov, Valentin M. *At Stalin's Side: His Interpreter's Memoirs from the October Revolution to the Fall of the Dictator's Empire*. New York: Birch Lane Press, 1994.
Beriya, Sergo. *Moi otets Lavrentii Beriya (My Father, Lavrenty Beria)*. Moscow: Sovremennik, 1994.
Blank, Stephen J. and Jacob W. Kipp. *The Soviet Military and the Future*. Westport, CT: Greenwood Press, 1992.
Brandt, M. Yu., et al. *Rossiya i mir. Uchebnaya kniga po istorii (Russia and the World: Textbook on History)*. Moscow: Vlados, 1994.
Cameron, Norman, R. H. Stevens, and H. R. Trevor-Roper (trans). *Hitler's Table Talk 1941–1944*. New York: Enigma Books, 2000.
Carr, E.H. *What Is History*. New York: Vintage Books, 1962.
———. *German-Soviet Relations Between the Two World Wars, 1919–1939*. New York: Arno Press, 1979.
Chamberlin, William Henry, ed. *Blueprint for World Conquest*. Washington, DC: Human Events, 1946.
Chaney, Otto Preston. *Zhukov*. Norman: University of Oklahoma Press, 1971.
Chubaryan, A. O. *V. I Lenin i formirovaniye sovetskoi vneshnei politiki (V. I. Lenin and the Formulation of Soviet Foreign Policy)*, Moscow: Nauka, 1972.

Chudeyev, Yu. V. *Rossiya Kitai: Strategichewskoye partnerstvo na sovremennom etape Problemy i perspektivy* (*Russia and China: Strategic Partnership at the Present Stage, Problems and Perspectives*), Moscow: Institute of Far Eastern Studies, Russian Academy of Sciences,2011.
Chuyev, Felix. *Sto sorok besed s Molotovym* (*140 Conversations with Molotov*), Moscow: Terra, 1991.
———. *Molotov Remembers: Inside Kremlin Politics, Conversations with Felix Chiuev* (Albert Resis, ed), Chicago: Ivan R. Dee, 1993.
Clausewitz, Carl. *On War*. Princeton, NJ: Princeton University Press, 1976.
Conquest, Robert. *The Great Terror A Reassessment*. New York: Oxford University Press, 1990.
———. *Stalin, Breaker of Nations*. New York: Penguin Books, 1991.
Crozier, Brian. *The Rise and Fall of the Soviet Empire*. Rockland, CA: Forum, 1999.
Dallin, David J. *Soviet Russia's Foreign Policy, 1939–1942*. New Haven, CT: Yale University Press, 1942.
Davies, Sarah, Harris, James (eds). *Stalin: A New History*. New York: Cambridge University Press, 2006.
Deane, John R. *The Strange Alliance: The Story of Our Efforts at Wartime Co-operation with Russia*. New York: Viking Press, 1947.
———. "Negotiating on Military Assistance, 1943–45," *Negotiating with the Russians*. Edited by Raymond Dennett and Joseph E. Johnson. Boston: World Peace Foundation, 1951.
Degras, Jane, ed. *The Communist International, 1919–1943: Documents*. Vols. 1–2. London: Oxford University Press, 1956–1960.
Deng Xiaoping. *Selected Works*. Vols. 1–3. Beijing: Foreign Languages Press, 1994.
Deriabin, Peter S. *Inside Stalin's Kremlin*. Washington, DC: Brassey's, 1998.
Deutsch, Harold and Showalter, Dennis (eds). *What If? Strategic Alternatives in WW II*. Chicago: The Emperor's Press, 1997.
Deutscher, Isaac. *Ironies of History*. New York: Oxford University Press, 1966.
Djilas, Milovan. *Conversations with Stalin*. New York: Harcourt Brace and Co., 1962.
Dolutskiy, I. I. *Obshchestvennaya istoriya XX vek* (*Fatherland History in the 20th Century*). Vols 1–2. Moscow: Mnemozinma 1002.
Donnelly, Christopher. *Red Banner The Soviet Military System in Peace and War*, London: Jane's Information Group, 1988.
Dulles, Foster Rhea. *The Road to Teheran: The Story of Russia and America, 1781–1943*. Princeton, NJ: Princeton University Press, 1944.
Dunne, Walter S., Jr. *Stalin's Keys to Victory: The Rebirth of the Red Army in WWII*. Mechanicsburg, PA: Stackpole Books 2006.
Dvoretsky, Lev. *Alien Wars: The Soviet Union's Aggressions Against the West*. Novato, CA: Presidio Press, 1996.
Dyakov, Yuri and Tatyana Bushuyeva. *Red Army and the Wehrmacht: How the Soviet Militarized Germany, 1922–1933, and Paved the Way for Fascism*. Amherst, NY: Prometheus Books, 1995.
Eissenstat, Bernard W. *Lenin and Leninism. State, Law and Society*. Lanham, MD: Lexington Books, 1971.
Erickson, John. *The Road to Stalingrad: Stalin's War with Germany*. Vol. 1, New Haven, CT: Yale University Press, 1975.
Erickson, John, and David Dilks. *Barbarossa: The Axis and the Allies*. Edinburgh: Edinburgh University Press, 1994.
Ericson, Edward E. III. *Feeding the German Eagle Soviet Economic Aid to Nazi Germany, 1933–1941*. Westport, CT: Prager, 1999.
Falin, V. M., ed. *Soviet Peace Efforts on the Eve of World War II*, 2 parts. Moscow: Novosti, 1973.
Federal Security Service and Foreign Intelligence Service, *Sekrety Gitlera na stole Stalina* (*Hitler's Secrets in Stalin's Desk*). Moscow: Mostoarkhiv, 1995.
Fest, Joachim. *Hitler*. New York: Random House, 1975.

Figes, Orlando. *The Whisperers: Private Life in Stalin's Russia*. New York: Henry Holt and Company, 2007.
Filippov, A. V. *Noveishaya istoriya Rossii, 1945–2006. Kniga dlya uchitelya* (*Newest History of Russia, 1945–2006. Book for the Teacher*). Moscow: Prosveshcheniye, 2007.
Fleming, D. F. *The Cold War and Its Origins, 1917–1950*. Vols. 1–2, Garden City, NY: Doubleday and Co., 1961.
Folly, Martin. *The United States and World War II: The Awakening Giant*. Edinburgh: Edinburgh University Press, 2002.
Fortunatov, V.V. *Otechestvennaya istoria dya gumanitarnikh institutov; Rekomendano nauchno-metodicheskim sovetom* (*Fatherland History for Institutes of the Humanities, recommended by the Scientific-Methodological Council*). St. Petersburg: Piter Press, 2009.
———. *Noveishaya istoriya Rossii v litsakh 1917–2008* (*Newest History of Russia as Seen Through Persons, 1917–2008*). St. Petersburg: Piter Press, 2009.
Friedberg, Aaron L. *A Contest for Supremacy: China, America, and the Struggle for Mastery in Asia*. New York: W.W. Norton, 2011.
Fugate, Bryan and Lev Dvoretsky. *Thunder on the Dnepr: Zhukov-Stalin and the Defeat of Hitler's Blitzkrieg*. Novato, CA: Presidio Press, 2001.
———. *Operation Barbarossa: Strategy and Tactics on the Eastern Front, 1941*. Novato, CA: Presidio Press, 1984.
Furet, Francois. *The Passing of an Illusion: The Idea of Communism in the Twentieth Century*. Chicago: University of Chicago Press, 1999.
Gaddis, John Lewis. *We Now Know: Rethinking Cold War History*. New York: Clarendon Press, 1998.
———. *George F. Kennan: An American Life*. New York: Penguin Press, 2011.
Gareyev, M. A. *M. V. Frunze—Voyenniy teoretik* (*M. V. Frunze: Military Theoretician*). Moscow: Voyenizdat, 1986.
Gellman, Barton D. *Contending with Kennan*. New York: Praeger, 1985.
Gellman, Irwin F. *Secret Affairs: Franklin Roosevelt, Cordell Hull, and Sumner Welles*. Baltimore, MD: Johns Hopkins University Press, 1995.
Getty, J. Arch and Oleg V. Naumov, *The Road to Terror: Stalin and the Self-Destruction of the Bolsheviks, 1932–1939*. New Haven, CT: Yale University Press, 2010.
Glantz, David M. *Stumbling Colossus The Red Army on the Eve of World War*. Lawrence: University Press of Kansas, 1998.
Glantz, David M. and Jonathan House. *When Titans Clash*. Lawrence: University Press of Kansas, 1995.
Glantz, Mary E. *FDR and the Soviet Union: The President's Battles Over Foreign Policy*. Lawrence: University Press of Kansas, 2005.
Goebbels, Josef. *The Early Goebbels Diaries 1925-1926*. New York: Praeger, 1962.
———. *Diaries 1939–1941*. New York: G. P. Putnam's Sons, 1982.
Goodman, Elliot R. *The Soviet Design for a World State*. New York: Columbia University Press, 1960.
Gosizdat. *Perepiski (Correspondence) Stalin, Roosevelt, Churchill, 1941–1945; 1944–1945*. 2 vols. Moscow: Gosizdat, 1957.
Gor'kov, Yuri. *Kreml', Stavka, Genshtab* (*Kremlin, High Command, and General Staff*). Tver, Russia: RIF Ltd., 1999.
Gorlizki, Yoram and Oleg Khlevniuk. *Cold Peace: Stalin and the Soviet Union's Ruling Circle, 1945–1953*. New York: Oxford University Press, 2004
Gormly, James L. *The Collapse of the Grand Alliance 1945–1948*. Baton Rouge: Louisiana State University Press, 1987.
Gorodetsky, Gabriel (ed). *Soviet Foreign Policy 1917–1991: A Retrospective*. London: Frank Cass, 1994.
Graebner, Norman et al. *America and the Cold War: A Realist Interpretation, 1941–1991*. New York: Praeger, 2010.
Hanhimaki, Jussi and Odd Arne Westad. *The Cold War: A History of Documents and Eyewitness Accounts*. New York: Oxford University Press, 2004

Hallas, Duncan. *The Comintern: A History of the Third International*. Chicago: Haymarket Books, 1985.
Halle, Louis J. *The Cold War as History*. New York: Harper and Row, 1967.
Harbutt, Fraser J. *The Iron Curtain: Churchill, America, and the Origins of the Cold War*. New York: Oxford University Press, 1986.
Hart, B.H. Liddell, *Strategy*, second ed. London: Meridian Books, 1967.
Haslam, Jonathan. *Russia's Cold War: From the October Revolution to the Fall of the Wall*. New Haven, CT: Yale University Press, 2011.
Haynes, John Earl and Harvey Klehr. *Venona: Decoding Soviet Espionage in America*. New Haven, CT: Yale University Press, 1999.
Hazard, John N. *The Soviet System of Government*. Chicago: University of Chicago Press, 1964.
Heller; Mikhail and Aleksandr Nekrich. *Utopia and Power: The History of the Soviet Union from 1917 to the Present*. New York: Summit Books, 1986.
Hillgruber, Andreas. *Germany and the Two World Wars*. Cambridge, MA: Harvard University Press, 1981.
Irving, David. *Goebbels: Mastermind of the Third Reich*. London: Focal Point, 1996.
Isayev, Aleksei, Zhitorchuk, Yuri, et al. *Velikaya Otechestvennaya katastrofiya II, 1941: Prichiny tragedii* (*The Fatherland's Great Catatrophe II: Reasons for the Tragedy*). Moscow: Yauza, 2007.
Kalugin, Oleg. *The First Directorate*. New York: St. Martin's Press, 1994.
Kennan, George F. *Russia and the West Under Lenin and Stalin*. Boswon: Little, Brown and Co., 1960.
Kershaw, Ian. *Fateful Choices: Ten Decisions that Changed the World, 1940–1941*, New York: Penguin Press, 2007.
Khrushchev, N. S. *The Crimes of the Stalin Era: Special Report to the 20th Congress of the Communist Party of the Soviet Union*, New York: New Leader Magazine, 1962.
———. *Khrushchev Remembers The Glasnost Tapes*. Boston: Little, Brown and Co., 1990.
Kokoshin, Andrei A. *Armiya I politika Sovetskaya voenno-politicheskaya i voyenno-strategicheskaya mysl', 1918–1991 gody* (*Army and Policy Soviet Military-Political and Military-Strategic Thought*). Moscow: Mezhdunarodniye Otnosheniya, 1995.
———. *Soviet Strategic Thought, 1917–91*. Cambridge, MA: MIT Press, 1995.
Krasnov, Valeriy. *Neizvestniy Zhukov* (*The Unknown Zhukov*). Moscow: Olma Press, 2000.
Krivitsky, Walter. *In Stalin's Secret Service*. Westport, CT: Hyperion Press, 1939.
Kuznetsov, N. G. *Kursom k pobede* (*On Course to Victory*). Moscow: Olma Press, 2003.
Laqueur, Walter. *Stalin Glasnost Revelations*. New York: Scribner's, 1990.
Latimer, Jon, *Deception in War: The Art of the Bluff, the Value of Deceit, and the Most Thrilling Episodes of Cunning in Military History, from the Trojan Horse to the Gulf War*. New York: The Overlook Press, 2001.
Leffler, Melvyn P. *The Specter of Communism: The United States and the Origins of the Cold War*. New York: Hill and Wang, 1994.
———. *For the Soul of Mankind: The United States and the Soviet Union and the Cold War*. New York: Hill and Wang, 2007.
Leffler, Melvyn P. and David S. Painter. *Origins of the Cold War: An International History*. New York: Routledge, 1994.
———. *A Preponderance of Power: National Security, the Truman Administration, and the Cold War*. Stanford, CA: Stanford University Press, 1992.
Leites, Nathan, *The Operational Code of the Politburo*. New York: McGraw-Hill, 1951.
———. *The Soviet Style in War*. New York: Crane Russak, 1982
———. *A Study of Bolshevism*. Glencoe, IL: The Free Press, 1953
Lenin, V. I. *Sochineniya*. Moscow: Ogiz, 1947
Librach, Jan. *The Rise of the Soviet Empire A Study of Soviet Foreign Policy*. New York: Prager, 1964
Lukacs, John. *June 1941: Hitler and Stalin*. New Haven, CT: Yale University Press, 2006.

Lukes, Igor. *Czechoslovakia Between Stalin and Hitler: The Diplomacy of Eduard Benes in the 1930s*. New York: Oxford University Press, 1996.
Malenkov, Andrei. *O moem otse George Malenkove (About My Father, Georgy Malenkov)*. Moscow: Tekhnoekos, 1992.
Martirorsyan, A. B. *Tragediya 1941 goda (The Tragedy of 1941)*. Moscow: Veche, 2008.
———. *Tragediya 22 iyunya: blitskrig ili izmena? (The Trasgedy of June 22: Blitzkrieg or Betrayal?)*. Moscow: Yauza, 2006.
———. *Na puti k mirovoi voine (On the Road to World War)*. Moscow: Veche, 2008.
———. *Stalin: biografiya vozhdya (Stalin: Biography of the Leader)*. Moscow: Veche, 2008.
———. *Stalin posle voiny, 1945–1953 (Stalin After the War, 1945-1953)*. Moscow: Veche, 2008.
———. *Stalin i velikaya otechestvennaya voina (Stalin and the Great Patriotic War)*. Moscow: Veche, 2008.
———. *Sto mifov o Berii: Vdokhnovitel' repressiy ili talantliviy organizator? 1917–1941 (Instigator of the Repressions or Talented Organizer? 1917-1953)*. Moscow: Veche, 2010.
Mastny, Vojtech, *Russia's Road to the Cold War*. New York: Columbia University Press, 1979.
Mel'tyukhov, Mikhail, Aleksandr Osokin, and Igor Pykhalov. *Tragediya 1941: Prichiny katastrofa (The Tragedy of 1941: Reasons for the Catastrophe)*. Moscow: Eksmo, 2008.
Menaul, Stewart, James E. Dornan et al. *Russian Military Power*. New York: St. Martin's, 1980.
Molotov, V. M. *Address to Constituents, Election Meeting February, 1946*. Soviet News, London, 1946.
Montefiore, Simon Sebag, *Stalin: The Court of the Red Tsar*. London: Weidenfeld and Nicolson, London, 2003.
Mosier, John. *Deathride: Hitler vs. Stalin on the Eastern Front, 1941–1945*. New York: Simon and Schuster, 2010.
Mukhin, Yuri. *Kto na camom dele razvyazal vtoruyu mirovuyu voinu? (Who Actually Started World War II?)* Moscow: Yayuza Press, 2009.
Müller, Rolf-Dieter and Gerd R. Ueberschäar. *Hitler's War in the East 1941–1945*. New York: Berghahn Books, 1997.
Murphy, David E. *What Stalin Knew: The Enigma of Barbarossa*. New Haven, CT: Yale University Press, 2005.
Narinskiy, N.M., S. Dembski. *Mezhdunarodniy krizis 1939 goda v traktovkakh rossiiskikh i pol'skih istorikov (The International Crisis of 1939 Through the Treatises of Russian and Polish Historians)*. Moscow: Aspect Press, 2009.
Nekrich, Aleksandr. *Pariahs, Predators, Partners German-Soviet Relations 1922–1941*. New York: Columbia University Press, 1997.
Nisbet, Robert. *Roosevelt and Stalin: The Failed Courtship*. New York: Regnery Gateway, 1988.
Orenstein, Harold S., trans. *Soviet Documents on the Use of War Experience*, vol. 1. London: Frank Cass, 1991.
Orenstein, Harold S and David M. Glantz. *Soviet Documents on the Use of War Experience*, Vol. 1. London: Frank Cass, 1991.
Ogarkov N. V., ed. *Voenniy entsiklopedicheskiy slovar' (Military Encyclopedia Dictionary)*. Moscow: Voennoye Izdatel'stvo 1986.
Ostrovskiy, V.P. and A. I. Utkin. *Istoriya Rossii XX vek (A History of Russia in the 20th Century)*. Moscow: Drofa, 1997.
Page, Stanley. *The Geopolitics of Leninism*. New York: Columbia University Press, 1982.
Paperno, A. *Tainy istorii (History's Secrets)*. Moscow: Terra-Knizhniy Klub, 1998.
Pauwell, Jaques R. *The Myth of the Good War: America in the Second World War*. Toronto: Lorimer and Co., 2002.
Pereslegin, Sergei. *Novaya istoriya vtoroi mirovoi (New History of the Second World War)*. Moscow: Eksmo, 2009.
Petrov, Vladimir. *June 22 1941: Soviet Historians and the German Invasion*. Columbia: University of South Carolina Press, 1968.

Pikhoya, Rudol'f. *SSSR: Istoriya velikoi imperii, pod znakom Stalina* (*USSR: History of the Great Empire, Under the Sign of Stalin*). St. Petersburg: Piter Press, 2009.
Pleshakov, Constantine. *The Secret History of the German Invasion of Russia, June 1941*, London: Weidenfeld and Nicolson, 2005.
Pons, Silvio. *Stalin and the Inevitable War, 1936–1941*. London: Frank Cass, 2002.
Possony, Stefan T. *Lenin The Compulsive Revolutionary*. London: George Allen amd Unwin, 1966.
Prados, John. *How the Cold War Ended: Debating and Doling History*. Washington, DC: Potomac Books, 2011.
Radzinsky, Edvard. *Stalin*. New York: Doubleday, 1996.
Raymond, Ellsworth. *The Soviet State*. New York: New York University Press, 1978.
Resis, Albert, ed. *Molotov Remembers: Conversations with Felix Chuev*. Chicago: Ivan R. Dee, 1993.
Roberts, Geoffrey. *The Soviet Union and the Origins of the Second World War Russo-German Relations and the Road to War, 1933–1941*. New York: St. Martin's Press, 1995.
———. *Stalin's Wars: From World War to Cold War, 1939–1953*. New Haven, CT: Yale University Press, 2006.
———. *Molotov: Stalin's Cold Warrior*. Washington, DC: Potomac Books, 2012.
Rogovin, Vadim. *Stalinskiy neonep* (*Stalin's Neo-NEP*). Moscow: BBK, 1994.
Rossi, A. *The Russo-German Alliance August 1939–June 1941* Boston: Beacon Press, 1951.
Rossiiskaya Akademiya Nauk (Russian Academy of Sciences). *Rossiya i Kitai: Izmeneniya v sotsial'noi strukture obshchestva)* (*Russia and China: Changes in the Social Structuring of Society*). Moscow: Russian Academy of Sciences, Noviy Khronograf, 2012.
———. *Kitai-Rossiya 2050: Strategiya Sorazvitiye* (*China and Russia: Strategy of Co-Development*). Moscow: Russian Academy of Sciences, 2006.
———. *Dukhovnaya kultura kitaya: Entsiklopediya* (*Spiritual Culture of China: Encyclopedia*). Moscow: Vostochnaya Literatura, Russian Academy of Sciences, 2009.
Rudzinski, Aleksander. *Soviet Peace Offensives*, New York: Carnegie Endowment for International Peace, 1953.
Sakharov, A. N., ed. *Sovetsko-pol'skiye otnosheniya v politicheskikh usloviyakh 30-kh godov XX stoletiya* (*Soviet-Polish Relations Under the Political Conditions of the 1930s in the Twentieth Century*). Moscow: Nauka, 2001.
Sarin, Oleg and Lev Dvoretsky. *Alien Wars: The Soviet Union's Aggressions Against the World, 1919–1939*. Novato, CA: Presidio Press, 1996.
Saul, Norman E. *Friends or Foes? The United States and Russia, 1921–1941*. Lawrence: University of Press of Kansas, 2005.
Schuman, Frederick L. *Russia Since 1917: Four Decades of Soviet Politics*, New York: Alfred A. Knopf, 1943.
———. *Soviet Politics at Home and Abroad*. New York: Alfred A. Knopf, 1947.
Scott, H. F. and William F. Scott. *The Armed Forces of the USSR*, second ed. Boulder, CO: Westview Press, 1981.
———. *Soviet Military Doctrine Continuity, Formulation, and Dissemination*. Boulder, CO: Westview Press, 1988.
———, eds. *The Soviet Art of War Doctrine, Strategy, and Tactics*. Boulder, CO: Westview Press, 1982.
Seaton, Albert. *Stalin as Military Commander*. New York: Praeger, 1975.
Service, Robert. *Stalin: A Biography*. Cambridge, MA: Belknap Press, 2005.
Shtemenko, S. M. *The Soviet General Staff at War, 1941–1945*, Book One. Moscow: Voenizdat, 1981.
Shulman, Marshall D. *Stalin's Foreign Policy: Reappraisal*. Cambridge, MA: Harvard University Press, 1963.
Simonov, Konstantin. *Glazami cheloveka moyego pokoleniya* (*Through the Eyes of a Man of My Generation*). Moscow: APN, 1988.
Sogrin, V. V. *Istoriya SShA Uchebnoye po sobiye* (*History of the USA School Textbook*). St. Petersburg: Piter Press, 2003.

Sokolovsky, V. D. *Voyennaya strategiya* (*Soviet Strategy*), 1st–2nd eds. Moscow: Izdatel'stvo Ministerstva Oborony SSSR, 1962–1963.
Soroko-Tsyupi, O. S. et al. *Mir v XX veke* (*The World in the 20th Century*), Russian history textbook for the 10th–11th grades. Moscow: Proveshcheniye, 1997.
Spahr, William J. *Stalin's Lieutenants A Study of Command Under Duress.* Novato, CA: Presidio Press, 1997.
Stalin, I. V. *Works*, The Hoover Institution, Stanford, 1967, 16 vols.
———. *Sochineniya* (*Works*), Ogiz, Moscow, 1947, 13 vols.
———. *On the Great Patriotic War of the Soviet Union.* Calcutta: Suren Dutt, 1975.
Sudoplatov, Pavel and Anatoli Sudoplatov. *Special Tasks.* Boston: Little, Brown and Co., 1994.
Sul'yanov, Anatoli. *Arestovat' v Kremlye O zhizne I smerti Marshala Berii* (*Arrested in the Kremlin On the Life and Death of Marshal Beriya*). Minsk, Belarus: MP Slavyanye, 1993.
Sun Tzu. *The Art of War.* New York: Oxford University Press, 1963.
Taubman, William. *Stalin's American Policy: From Entente to Detente to Cold War.* New York: W.W. Norton, 1982.
Tokaev, G. A. *Stalin's War.* London: Weidenfeld and Nicolson, 1951.
Tolstoy, Nikolai. *Stalin's Secret War.* New York: Holt, Rinehart and Winston, 1981.
Topitsch, Ernst. *Stalin's War A Radical New Theory on the Origins of the Second World War.* New York: St. Martin's Press, 1987.
Towster, Julian. *Political Power in the USSR, 1917–1947.* New York: Oxford University Press, 1948.
Tucker, Robert C. *Stalin in Power The Revolution from Above, 1928–1941.* New York: W. W. Norton, 1992.
———. *The Soviet Political Mind: Stalinism and Post-Stalin Change.* New York: W.W. Norton, 1971.
Utkin, A. I. *Rossiya i zapad* (*Russia and the West*), school textbook. Moscow: Gadariki, 2000.
———. *Mirovaya kholodnaya voina* (*Global Cold War*). Moscow: Eksmo, 2005.
Vdovin, A. I. *Istoriya SSSR ot Lenina do Gorbacheva* (*History of the USSR from Lenin to Gorbachev*). Moscow: Vechi, 2011.
Verkhovsky, Yakov and Valentina Tyrmos. *Stalin: Tainiy 'tsenariy' nachala voiny* (*Secret 'Scenario' of the Start of the War*). Moscow: Olma Press, 2006.
Vigor, P. J. *The Soviet View of War, Peace, and Neutrality.* London: Routledge and Kegan Paul, 1975.
Volkogonov, Dmitri. *Stalin: Triumph and Tragedy.* Rocklin, CA: Prima Publishing, 1991.
———. *Autopsy for an Empire: The Seven Leaders Who Built the Soviet Regime.* Glencoe, IL: The Free Press, 1998.
———. *Lenin: A New Biography.* Glencoe, IL: The Free Press, 1994.
Vyshinsky, Andrei A. *The Law of the Soviet State.* New York: MacMillan, 1948.
Vyshlev, O. V. *Hakanunye 22 iyuniya 1941 goda* (*On the Eve of June 22, 1941*). Moscow: Hauka, 2001.
Walker, Martin. *The Cold War: A History.* New York: Henry Holt, 1993.
Weeks, Albert L. *The Other Side of Coexistence: An Analysis of Russian Foreign Policy.* New York: Pitman, 1970.
———. *The Troubled Détente.* New York: New York University Press, 1976.
———. *Soviet and Communist Quotations.* New York: Pergamon-Brassey's, 1987.
———. *Stalin's Other War: Soviet Grand Strategy, 1939–1941.* Lanham, MD: Rowman and Littlefield, 2002.
———. *Russia's Life-Saver: Lend-Lease Aid to the USSR in World War II*, Lanham, MD: Lexington Books, 2004.
———. *The Choice of War: Iraq and the Just War Tradition.* New York: Praeger, 2009.
———. *Assured Victory: How "Stalin the Great" Won the War But Lost the Peace.* New York: Praeger, 2011
Werth, Alexander, *Russia at War, 1941–1945.* New York: Dutton, 1964.

Westad, Odd Arne, *Reviewing the Cold War: Approaches, Interpretations, Theory*. London: Frank Cass, 2000
Whaley, Barton. *Codeword Barbarossa*. Cambridge, MA: MIT Press, 1975.
Whelan, John G. *Soviet Diplomacy and Negotiating Behavior: The Emerging New Context for U.S. Diplomacy*. Boulder, CO: Westview Press, 1983.
Woodward, Llewelllyn, *British Foreign Policy in the Second World War*. London: Her Majesty's Stationery Office, 1962.
Yakovlev, A. N., ed. *Rossiya. XX vek 1941 god Dokumenty v 2-kh knigakh (Russia 20th Century The Year 1941. Documents. In Two Books)*. Moscow: Mezhdunarodniy Fond "Demokratiya," 1998.
Yur'ev, A. I. *Noveishaya istoriya Rossii, Fevral' 1917 g-nachalo XXI (Newest History of Russia (February 1917 to the Beginning of the 21st Century)*. Moscow: Giperboreya, 2010.
Zagladin, N. V. *Vsemirnaya istoriya XX vek (World History in the 20th Century)*, Uchebnik (Textbook). Moscow: Russkoye Slovo, 2004.
Zakoretskiy, Keistut. *Tret' ya mirovaya voina Stalina (Stalin's Third World War)*. Moscow: Yauza Press, 2009.
Zhilin, P. A. *Istoriya voyennovo iskusstva (History of Military Art)*, Officer's Library Series. Moscow: Voyenizdat, 1986.
Zhukov, Georgi K. *Vospominaniya i razmyshleniya (Reminiscences and Reflections)*. Vols. 1–3. Moscow: Novosti Publishers, 1990.
Zubok, Vladislav M. A., *Failed Empire: The Soviet Union in the Cold War from Stalin to Gorbachev*. Chapel Hill: University of North Carolina Press, 2007.
Zubok, Valdislav M. A. and Constantine Pleshakov, *Inside the Kremlin's Cold War from Stalin to Khrushchev*. Cambridge, MA: Harvard University Press, 1996.

ARTICLES

Batayeva, T. V. *Uchebnik po istorii: orientiry i adresati* ("Textbook on History: Guides and Addressees"), *Prepodavaniye istorii v shkole*, No. 4, 1998, pp. 46–56.
Bezymenskii, Lev A. *Sovetskaya razvedka pered voinoi* ("Soviet Intelligence
Bobylev, Pavel N. *Tochku v diskussii stavit' rano. K voprosu o planirovanii v general'nom shtabe RKKA vozmozhnoi voiny s Germaniye v 1940–1941 godakh* ("Calling an Early Halt to the Discussion About the Problem in the General Staff of the RKKA on Planning a Possible War with Germany from the Years 1940–1941"), *Otechesvennaya istoriya*, No. 1, 2000, pp. 41–64.
Chernyak, Aleksandr. *O nashei velikoi pobede* ("About Our Great Victory"), *Pravda*, April 12, 1995.
Dmitriev, V. *Diplomatiya i voyennaya strategiya* ("Diplomacy and Military Strategy"), Voyennaya mysl', No. 7, July 1971, p. 51.
Dziak, John. Soviet Perceptions of Military Power: The Interaction of Theory and Practice, National Strategy Information Center, Inc., Crane, Rusaak & Company, Inc., N.Y., 1981.
V.V. Farsobin. *U. Cherchiill', Muskuly mira (W. Churchill, Muscles of Peace)*, book review of Churchill's writings, *Voprosy Istorrii*, No. 1, 2004, pp. 171–173.
Gilensen, V. M., *Fatal'naya oshibka* ("The Fatal Mistake"), *Voyenno-istoricheskii zhurnal*, No. 4, pp. 25–35, 1998.
Goffman, Ioakhim (Hoffman, Joachim). *Podgotovka Sovetskovo Soyuza knastupatel'noi voine* ("Preparation by the Soviet Union for Offensive War"), *Otechestvennaya istoriya*, No. 47, 1993, pp. 19–31.
Gor'kov, Yu. A. *Gotovil li Stalin uprezhdayushchii udar protiv Gitlera v 1941 g.?* ("Did Stalin Plan a Preemptive Strike Against Hitler in 1941?"), *Novaya I noveishaya istoriya*, 1993, No. 3, pp. 29–45.
Historicus. "Stalin on Revolution," *Foreign Affairs*, January 1949, pp. 175–214.

Bibliography

Kells, Robert E. Capt. US Army, "Intelligence, Doctrine and Decision-making," Military Intelligence, July-September 1985.

Jacob W. Kipp. "Barbarossa, Soviet Covering Forces and the Initial Period of War: Military History and Airland Battle,"Available at http://fmso.leavenworth.army.mil/documents/barbaros.htm

———. *Foresight and Forecasting: The Russian and Soviet Military Experience.* College Station, Texas: Center for Strategic Technology Stratech Studies, 1988.

———. "Lenin and Clausewitz: The Militarization of Marxism," *Military Affairs*, XLIX, No. 4, (December 1985), 184-191.

———. "Barbarossa, Soviet Covering Forces and the Initial Period of War: Military History and AirLand Battle," *The Journal of Soviet Military Studies*, I, No. 2 (June 1988), 188–212. The article originally appeared here. There is a great deal of useful material on GPW in this journal, now called *The Journal of Slavic Military Studies*.

———. "Blitzkrieg in Crisis: Barbarossa and the Battle of Smolensk," *Soviet and Post-Soviet Review*, 19, No. 1–3 (1992), 91–136. [Special number edited by David Holloway].

Jacob. W. Kipp. "Mass, Mobility and the Origins of Soviet Operational Art" in Karl Reddel, ed., *Transformation in Russian and Soviet Military History: Proceedings of the Twelfth Military History Symposium*, USAF Academy, 1986. Washington, DC: United States Air Force Office of Air Force History, 1990, 87–116.

———. "General-Major A. A. Svechin and Modern War: Military History and Military Theory," Introductory essay for: Kent Lee, editor, A. A. Svechin, *Strategy*. Minneapolis: East View Publications, 1992, 21–60.

———. "Two Views of Warsaw: The Russian Civil War and Soviet Operational Art, 1920–1930," in: B. J. C. McKercher and Michael A. Hennessy, eds., *The Operational Art: Developments in the Theories of War*. West Port, CT: Praeger, 1996, 51–86.

Lenin, V.I. *Ya proshu zapisyvat' menshe; eto ne dol'zhno popadat' v pechat'* (I Propose Writing Less and Not Reproducing This in the Press), *Istoricheskii* Arkhiv, No. 1, 1992, pp. 12–30.

Lyulechnik, V. "*A k voine my gotovilis' I byli gotovy…*" (Yes, We Were Prepared and Were Prepared for War.."), *Panorama*, May 8-14, 1996.

———. *Nakanune i v gody voiny* ("On the Eve and During the Years of the War"), *Panorama*, June 18–24, 1997.

Mar'ina, Valentin B. *Dnevnik G. Dimitrova* (G. Dimitrov's Diary), *Voprosy istorii*, No. 7, 2000, pp. 32–54.

Markoff, Alexei (Gen.). "Stalin's War Plans," *Saturday Evening Post*, Sept. 20, 1952.

Mel'tyukhov, Mikhail I. *Narashchivaniye sovetskovo voyennovo prisutstviya v Pribaltike v 1939–1941 godakh* ("The Growing Soviet Military Presence in the Baltic Region in the Years 1939–1941"), *Otechestvennaya istoriya*, No. 4, 1999, pp. 46–70.

Mr. X [George F. Kennan]. "The Sources of Soviet Conduct," *Foreign Affairs*, January 1949, pp. 566–582.

Ogarkov, N. V. "History Teaches Vigilance," Foreign Broadcast Information Service, Aug. 30, 1985.

———. "The Defense of Socialism: Experience of History and the Contemporary World," Red Star, May 9, 1984.

Plimak, Yevgenii, Antonov, Vadim. "Stalin znal, shto delal" ("Stalin Knew What He Was doing"), *Moskovskiye novosti*, Mar. 10–17, 1996.

Raack, R.C. "Stalin's Plans for World War II," Journal of Contemporary History, No. 26, 1991, pp. 215–227.

———. "Stalin's role in the Coming of World War II," *World Affairs*, Spring 1996, Washington, D.C., 1996, pp. 1–18.

Rogovin, Vadim. *Stalinskiy neonep* (Stalin's Neo-NEP), BBK, Moscow, 1994.

Sejna, Jan. We Will Bury You, Sidgwick & Jackson, London, 1982.

Shevelev, Lev. "Stalin and the Nuremberg Trial," Interview with Historian Natalya Lebedeva, *Moscow News*, No. 11, Mar. 24–30, 1995.

Volkogonov, Dmitri. Mir—eto tsel', kotoraya dostigayetsya lish' soobshcha ("Peace Was an Goal Achieved Only Jointly"), *Rossiiskiye vesti,* Jan. 12, 1995.

Weeks, Albert L. "The Garthoff-Pipes Debate on Soviet Doctrine: Another Perspective, *Strategic Review,* Winter 1983, pp. 57–64.

———. "The Soviet View Toward Prognostication," *Military Review,* September 1983, pp. 49–57.

———. "Soviet Military Doctrine," *Global Affairs,* Winter, 1988, pp. 170–187.

———. "The Soviet Defense Council," *Defense & Diplomacy,* May 1990, pp. 42–7.

———. "Russia Unfurls Its New/Old Military Doctrine," *The Officer, ROA National Security Report,* January 1994, pp. 30, 35.

GOVERNMENT DOCUMENTS

Nazi-Soviet Relations 1939–1941, U.S. Department of State, 1948.
Soviet Political Agreements and Results, Staff Study, Committee on the Judiciary, U.S. Senate, 86th Congress, 1959.
Soviet Diplomacy and Negotiating Behavior, Committee on Foreign Relations, U.S. House of Representatives, 96th Congress, Vol. 1, 1979.

About the Author

Albert L. Weeks is the author of several books on international affairs and many articles published in civilian and military periodicals from *The New York Times* and *Christian Science Monitor* to U.S. Armed Forces and Intelligence Journals.

Weeks served in the U.S. Department of State as Senior Soviet Analyst during the Cold War. He oversaw research for international broadcasting from Europe from 1950–57. In this sense, as a "Cold-Warrior," he had first-hand experience dealing with Cold War issue. As a result, his perspectives were broadened by this experience and expertise. Weeks is convinced that a new Cold War with "another Soviet Union" can be avoided, or if it came about, could be more soundly interpreted than the one that broke out after World War II.